The Stargazer's Bible

Also by W. S. Kals

PRACTICAL BOATING
PRACTICAL NAVIGATION
HOW TO READ THE NIGHT SKY
THE RIDDLE OF THE WINDS

The Stargazer's Bible

By W. S. KALS

Illustrated by the Author

DOUBLEDAY

NEW YORK   LONDON   TORONTO   SYDNEY   AUCKLAND

Published by Doubleday, a division of Bantam Doubleday Dell Publishing
Group, Inc., 666 Fifth Avenue, New York, New York 10103.

DOUBLEDAY and the portrayal of an anchor with a dolphin are trademarks
of Doubleday, a division of Bantam Doubleday Dell Publishing Group, Inc.

The constellation designs based on H. A. Rey's presentation are from *The Stars: A New Way to
See Them,* copyright © 1952, 1962, 1967 and 1970 by H. A. Rey and used by permission of the
publishers, Houghton Mifflin Company.

Library of Congress Cataloging in Publication Data

Kals, W. S.
  The stargazer's bible.

  Includes index.
  1. Astronomy—Observers' manuals.   I. Title.
QB64.K34   523

Contents

setups: camera carried piggyback on guiding telescope; camera without lens attached in place of eyepiece (primary-focus method); camera with lens where your eye normally would be (afocal method); and camera without lens, some distance from eyepiece (projection method).

PART ONE

Naked-eye Stargazing

1

Stargazing in North America, Europe, Etc.

People from scout age to retirees would come up to me at the planetarium of which I was the director and ask, "How can I learn the stars and constellations?" It was never said, but I soon found out: They all wanted a quick and, if possible, an easy method.

By "learning" they meant acquiring the ability to name stars and constellations they saw in the sky—as you identify a robin—or to find one whose name they knew—as you pick a daisy, not a dandelion, when you are asked to get a bunch of daisies.

By "stars" they meant, of course, not *all* stars but the brightest ones. And not only what astronomers call stars: that is, distant bodies that, like the sun, shine by their own light. These people included the handful of planets, nearby bodies that, like Earth, circle the sun and reflect its light. To the naked eye they look like stars, often very bright stars.

These planets wander among the stars, which seem fixed in relation to one another.

The *fixed stars* actually zip through space in all directions. But they are so unimaginably far away that in one lifetime, or even many lifetimes, we don't notice any shift in the patterns they form, the *constellations*. Grouping stars into constellations reduces the large number of stars to a much smaller number of patterns.

On a moonless night, away from human lights, you may see some two or three thousand stars. Compare that with, at most, eighty-eight constellations. To see all eighty-eight you'd have to watch the sky in all seasons and not just from the Northern Hemisphere.

Learning the constellations sounds like a good way to "learn the stars." And you can reduce their number by learning just the constellations visible where you are.

But there are difficulties. Some constellations are themselves hard to find; many constellations become unrecognizable in moonlight or in the glow of distant city lights. To recognize a constellation that's only partly above the horizon, you'd have to memorize not only the individual constellations, but also how they all fit together.

Star maps and star finders provide limited help. You'll read about them in Chapter 8.

You don't see the stars and constellations move—just as you don't see the sun move. But look a little later in the same night, and they are higher or lower in the sky and are more to the west (or in parts of the sky, more to the east). Look a few months later, and familiar constellations have disappeared while some others have become visible. Both the nightly movement and the seasonal changes are not the stars' doing but—as you probably know—the result of the motion of Earth.

If you travel west or east—say from Philadelphia to Denver, or the other way—nothing much changes in your night sky. You get a rebroadcast of your show to accommo-date your local time. The star show aired at 9 P.M. Eastern Standard Time in Philadelphia will also be aired at 9 P.M. Mountain Standard Time in Denver.

But travel south—say from Cleveland to Key West—and some characters in the sky show change. That all-season favorite the Big Dipper may be on vacation, and new stars appear in Key West. At the right time you may even get a glimpse of the Southern Cross!

What you need is a way to show where bright stars and conspicuous constellations are in *your* sky at any time of the night, and any night of the year. (They will be in the same position at the same date and time next year, and the next.)

You will also want to be able to find or identify the planets that are visible to the naked eye but will *not* be in the same positions next year.

A few years ago I published a system that

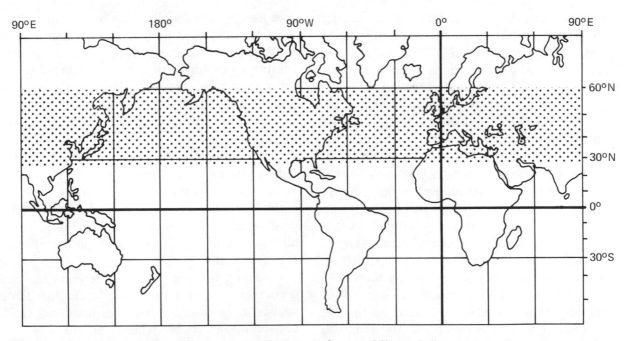

Fig. 1. Map of the world. The heavy horizontal line, labeled 0°, is the equator; figures at right indicate latitude north or south of the equator. The heavy vertical line, labeled 0°, is the meridian of Greenwich; figures at top indicate longitude west or east of Greenwich.

The shaded part shows the area under discussion. (For other areas, see Chapter 9.)

did all these things for the most populated areas of the Northern Hemisphere (*How to Read the Night Sky* [Doubleday]).

In the book you are now holding, I start again with that area, where most of my readers are likely to live. Then, to help stargazers—travelers and residents—in the Tropics and the Southern Hemisphere, I'll adapt the system to those areas in Chapter 9.

I'll supply you with two sky maps in the original coverage area, a third for areas south of it. You'll align these maps with the sky at your location according to instructions. For that you'll use only one simple tool: one of your hands. (You may find a flashlight handy to refer to the book. It won't spoil your night vision if you use a red bulb or put red cellophane over its lens.)

Only bright stars and star patterns that remain visible on a full-moon night are shown on these maps. But once you have mastered the basic technique you can find or identify *all* stars visible to the naked eye, and even objects you can see only through binoculars or a telescope.

In the next few pages you'll be introduced to a few technical terms. And you'll have to do some concentrated thinking. But no one ever found learning the stars easy.

A Basic Star Map

Wherever you may be out of doors, the sky—by day or by night—gives the appearance of a dome, the upper half of a sphere with you at the center. That dome seems to rest on your *horizon,* the circle all around you where sky and water, or sky and flat land, appear to meet.

Moon, sun, and stars seem attached to the dome of the sky.

That, of course, is an illusion. The moon is quite close to us, only 30 Earth diameters away. The sun is 400 times farther. The nearest star is about 300,000 times farther from us than the sun; other bright stars you

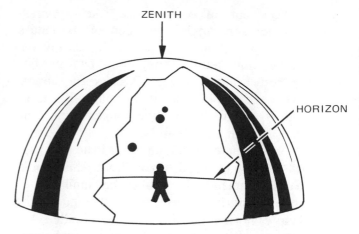

Fig. 2. The dome of the sky.

see may be another thousand times more distant.

The point directly above you is your *zenith*. If you measured the angle between your horizon and your zenith you'd get 90 degrees, whether you measured from the point east of you, south of you, or wherever.

A star a third of the way up between your horizon and your zenith would then be 30 degrees above your horizon. You can measure that angle with your hand; keeping your arm outstretched, you'll get about three hands.

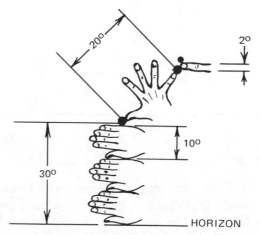

Fig. 3. Measuring in the sky: Held at arm's length from the eye, one finger covers 2° in the sky; one hand (palm and thumb) covers 10°; one span (fingers spread) covers 20°.

You can also measure the *apparent distance*—the angle—between any two stars in fingers (about 2 degrees), hands (10 degrees), and spans (20 degrees). That method (which I didn't invent) works for almost everyone. The reason: People with large hands are likely to have longer arms than people with small hands.

Now let me introduce you to the first type of star map used throughout this book. You'll immediately notice the similarity to the map of (much of) the world (Fig. 1). The heavy horizontal line is again called the equator. When it is necessary to distinguish it from the equator on Earth, the equator in the sky is called the *celestial equator*.

Ancient astronomers gave the name "latitude" to another measurement in the sky, so a different term is used to measure what would be latitude on a globe. The term is *declination,* abbreviated DEC. Corresponding to the parallels (of latitude) on the globe are the circles of declination. Like latitude, declination is labeled north (N) or south (S) of the equator.

The term "longitude" again having been preempted, astronomers call what corresponds to longitude on a globe *right ascension,* abbreviated RA. Unlike longitude, which is measured both east and west of Greenwich, right ascension is measured straight through with the numbers increasing toward the east, from 0 to 360 degrees. You'll see very shortly why it is often convenient to use hours (from 0 to 24) instead of degrees. That's the system you'll find throughout this book.

Astronomers give RA in hours, minutes, and seconds. In this book you'll find rough measurements expressed in fractions or decimals. What the astronomer would write as $7^h30^m00^s$ will be given as $7\frac{1}{2}^h$ or 7.5^h.

The practice of expressing right ascension in hours gives the half circles that correspond to the meridians of longitude on a globe the name *hour circles.* Since in this and other drawings they appear as straight lines, I may refer to them as *hour lines.*

The heavy vertical line (right ascension 0° or 0^h) corresponds to the meridian of Greenwich (longitude 0°).

The point where it crosses the celestial

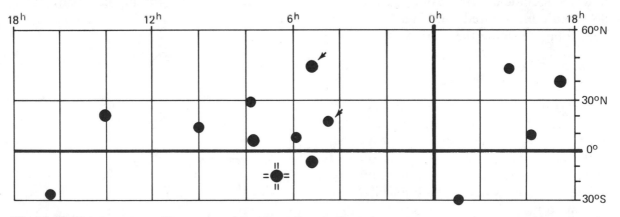

Fig. 4. Basic star map. Compare with map of the world (Fig. 1). The heavy horizontal line, labeled 0°, is the *celestial equator;* figures at right indicate *declination* north or south. The heavy vertical line, labeled 0°, is the zero hour circle; figures at top indicate *right ascension* (RA), measured in hours (1 hour = 15°).

Stars are shown by dots: the brighter the star, the larger the dot. (Sirius, the brightest star, has double rays added.)

You can measure the approximate angle between stars by using the scale on the right. *Example:* The stars to which the arrows point are about 35°, $3\frac{1}{2}$ hands, apart.

equator (DEC 0°, RA 0ʰ) has several names: the *vernal equinox,* often shortened to the *equinox;* as navigators call it, the *First Point of Aries* or, more briefly, just *Aries.* No star marks its location. It is simply a reference point near where the sun crosses the celestial equator at the beginning of spring; and it is no longer in the constellation Aries but in Pisces, moving toward Aquarius.

Our next job is to find how such a star map shows stars where you are watching them.

The Star Map and Your Latitude

The imaginary circle of the celestial equator will be your reference line. Everywhere on Earth (except the North Pole and the South Pole, where the equator lies on your horizon) you'll see only one half of that circle. And everywhere on Earth—except the poles—it crosses your horizon exactly east and west of you. In north latitudes it reaches its highest point exactly south of you. How high that point is above your southern horizon depends on your latitude.

If you can find your location on the map (Fig. 6), you can read your latitude at the right margin to the nearest degree, which is more than accurate enough. Anywhere else,

you can get it from any atlas or a map, always at the right or left margin.

If you already recognize Polaris, the polestar, measure how many degrees it is above your horizon. Whatever angle you get is—close enough—your latitude. In Winnipeg you'll get about five hands. Your latitude is 50 degrees.

To locate the high point of the celestial equator in your sky, you'll have to know where south is. If you used Polaris for finding your latitude, you already know that. Polaris is virtually due north, so south is in exactly the opposite direction.

Your town may be laid out so that streets or avenues run north–south. In open country a road map will often help. Turn the map until it agrees with the landscape. Its bottom edge is now south.

If you use a compass to find south, remember that in most places the compass needle does not point to true north. In the United States you could be up to 20 degrees off, either east or west of north. A local scout should be able to tell you how much and in which direction to correct.

By whatever means you got your latitude and south, you can now trace the celestial equator in your night sky.

ONE: Face south. East will then be left of you, west right of you.
TWO: Subtract your latitude from 90 degrees. Measure the resulting angle up from your south point. (That is the same as measuring your latitude down from the

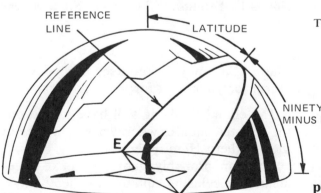

Fig. 5. Matching the basic star map to the dome of the sky. Our reference line, the celestial equator, goes through the east and west

points on your horizon and rises highest south of you. At that point it will be as many degrees below your zenith as you are north of the equator. In latitude 40°N it will be 40° (four hands) below the point directly above you.

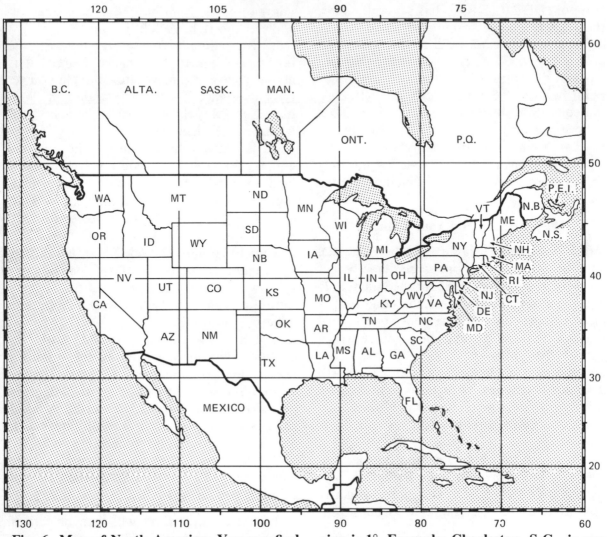

Fig. 6. Map of North America. You can find your latitude from the right margin, where every tenth degree is labeled; each small divi- sion is 1°. Example: Charleston, S.C., is near 33°.

zenith, which is 90 degrees above your horizon. And it's easier.) Fix the spot in your mind—by its distance from a nearby star, a void between two stars. . . .

THREE: With outstretched arm, give that spot a Roman salute. Now swing your arm far right until it points to the west point on your horizon. Bring it back to the spot you memorized moments ago. Now swing it left, to the east point on your horizon. The Roman salute implies use of your right

arm. You may, of course, use your left arm; or your right for west, left for east.

The complete swing will have traced out the celestial equator wherever you may be in the Northern Hemisphere.

You can probably guess the next statement: The celestial equator, the heavy horizontal line on the star map, must somehow fit over the line your arm has just traced in the sky.

The star map, like the corresponding map

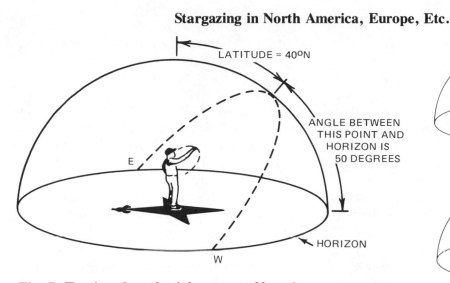

Fig. 7. Tracing the celestial equator. Note the change in angle above the horizon in different latitudes.

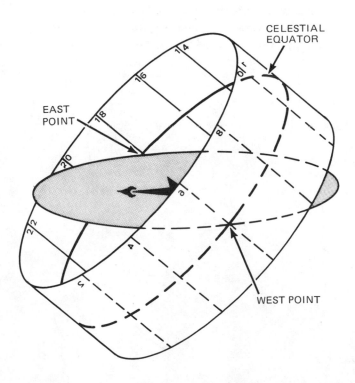

Fig. 8. The basic star map, joined at the ends to form a ring, placed over your horizon.

of the world, should be thought of as a ring. The star map should be joined at the two 18^h lines, the geographic map at longitude 90°E.

The Basic Star Map, Time, and Date

Half of the joined-at-the-ends star map at any given moment will be below your horizon.

Which part of the star map is now above the horizon, and what stars are visible? That's best solved with a concept probably new to you: *star time*. If you like long words, you can call it *sidereal time*. Either way it is expressed in hours, from 0^h to 24^h.

When star time at your location (local sidereal time) is 12^h, the line marked 12^h on the star map will be due south of you. It will be straight up from the south point on your horizon, pointing toward your zenith.

You see at any one time only one half of the joined star map, 12 of the 24^h of right ascension. At 12^h, the line marked 18^h will be sloping upward east (left) of you. More specifically, its point on the equator will be due east of you on your horizon.

The line marked 6^h will be west (right) of you. The point where it cuts the celestial equator will be exactly west of you and on your horizon.

About an hour later, your star time will be 13ʰ. Now the 13ʰ line is straight up, due south of you. The 19ʰ line (13 + 6ʰ) will be due east of you (equator on the east point of your horizon). The 7ʰ line (13 − 6ʰ) will be due west of you, again with the equator on your horizon.

You can see now why it is handy to label the right ascension lines in hours rather than in degrees.

But why bother with star time when it increases by one hour every hour? I didn't say it did. I said ''about an hour later.'' Actually, the interval is 59 minutes 50 seconds. That sounds like a quibble. For aligning a star map to a line measured with your hand, and to a south found by road map, a time difference of 10 seconds couldn't matter less.

But they add up. In one day they add up to four minutes—still unimportant for our purpose. But in one week, that makes star time gain about a half hour on our normal clock. In a month, star time gains about two hours.

At the beginning of autumn, our usual time and star time are the same. But from then on, star time gains at the rate of one hour every two weeks.

You may wonder where the difference in time comes from. The earth rotates around its axis once in about 23ʰ56ᵐ. Why, then, do we use a day of 24ʰ00ᵐ? Because our daily lives are geared to the sun. The interval from one noon to the next, averaged over the year, works out to 24 hours exactly. The interval is longer than the period of rotation of Earth because Earth, besides rotating around its axis, also travels around the sun.

The slippage between civil time (sun time) and star time explains the disappearance of some constellations from the night sky as the seasons change. The stars operate on star time; the night is governed by the sun-based time.

For a simple example, consider a star on the celestial equator—one of the stars in the constellation Orion, for instance. In mid-December, that star bears south of you at midnight local time, having risen at 6 P.M.

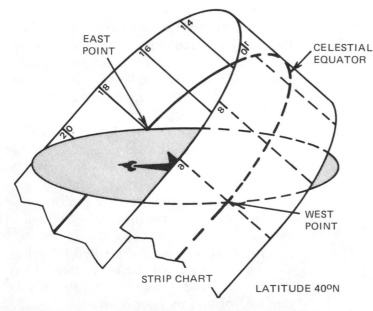

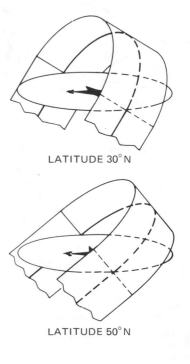

Fig. 9. The strip of the basic star map, placed according to your latitude.

and being due to set at 6 A.M. tomorrow. You'll see that star from dusk to dawn. At the rate of one hour every two weeks, that star will rise and set two hours earlier each month. By mid-June the star will then rise by 6 A.M., bear south of you at noon, and set by 6 P.M. All of that is during daylight hours, so you won't see the star at all.

To align the basic star chart to your sky, you need to know the approximate star time. Calculating how many days, or weeks, or months have elapsed since the last beginning of autumn, and adding the needed correction, is awkward.

A simpler method is to look up the star time in a table (Fig. 10).

ONE: Find the line of the nearest date.
TWO: Find the column of the hour of standard time you want, evening, midnight, or morning hour. (Daylight Saving Time is fast time. To get standard time, subtract one hour.)
THREE: On the line of the nearest date, in the column of the hour, read the star time.
FOUR: If you want the star time for one half hour later, add ½ hour.

The star time you have found will be accurate enough to align your star chart.

Once you become familiar with some stars

Date	Evening Hours						Mid-night	Morning	
	6	7	8	9	10	11		1	2
Mar. 7	5	6	7	8	9	10	11	12	
15	5½	6½	7½	8½	9½	10½	11½		
22	6	7	8	9	10	11	12		
30	6½	7½	8½	9½	10½				

Fig. 10. Star time (complete table shown on pages 134–135). *Example:* At midnight on March 22 (or near that time or date), use star time 12^h.

and star patterns, you will not need to look up star time in a table. You'll read it directly from the stars.

For now, trace the equator in the sky and imagine the star map bowed over your horizon with the line corresponding to present star time south of you. The dots on the map will then approximately match the brightest fixed stars visible at your location at this time.

You may see one or more bright "stars" not shown on the basic map. They are planets. In later chapters you'll see how the same star map helps you find or identify the planets.

2

The Twenty-one Brightest Stars

In learning to identify or find stars, it is logical to begin with the brightest ones. There are only twenty-one stars brighter than second magnitude. (Magnitude here has nothing to do with the size of a star. It is simply a measure of a star's brightness as seen from Earth.)

If you live north of latitude 35°N you will see only fifteen of these stars. Figure 6 shows what parts of North America are north of that line. All Europe is north of it. For the rest of the world, refer to Figure 1. These fifteen stars are the ones shown on the basic star map, Figure 4.

All these stars have names; some, rather strange names. You may need help with their pronunciation but may not want to struggle with a complicated system such as dictionaries use. Here is the key used in this book:

1. The stressed syllable is printed in small capital letters.

2. Short vowels:
   a as in *fat*
   e as in *wet*
   i as in *it*
   o as in *odd*
   uh as in *up*
   The *uh* is used also for the neutral sound we use in unstressed syllables in such words as sof*a*, kitt*e*n, penc*i*l, lem*o*n, and circ*u*s, as well as the vowel sound in *irk* and *urn*.

3. Long vowels:
   ay as in *fare*
   ee as in *feet*
   eye as in *ice*
   oh as in *go*
   you as in *use*
   oo as in *food*
   You may notice that the first five of these have the sounds of the names of the letters *a, e, i, o,* and *u.*

I'll give the phonetic spelling of stars and

constellations the first time they appear and repeat it for your convenience in some lists.

This rather simple code will get you close to the accepted pronunciation. Unfortunately, some of the names have more than one. *Example:* Betelgeuse (BET-el-juhrz). The last vowel is also sounded like the long German umlaut *ö,* as in *schön* or Köln, or made to rhyme with *ewes.* Sailors ignore all dictionaries, which give a few more variations, and call it "beetle juice."

I'll do more than just give you names and help you pronounce them. I'll group all but one of the fifteen stars into a few patterns. You could call them *superconstellations.*

Superconstellations

THE HEXAGON: Betelgeuse (BET-el-juhrz) near the equator at 6^h is surrounded by a battered hexagon of bright stars. That hexagon is about six hands high, five hands wide. Clockwise from the top the stars that frame Betelgeuse are:

Capella	(kuh-PELL-uh)
Aldebaran	(al-DEB-er-an)
Rigel	(REYE-juhl)
Sirius	(SI-ri-uhs)
Procyon	(PROH-see-uhn) and
Pollux	(POL-luhks)

To help me remember these star names in the right order, I've made up a silly jingle. I think of a difficult ship's captain who insists that the rigging be polished. Now the first mate reports:

"CAPtain, ALL DE RIGging SEEms
PROperly POLished."

That reminds me of Capella, Aldebaran, Rigel, Sirius, Procyon, and Pollux.

THE DOUBLE TRIANGLE: Centered on the equator and the 14^h line are two triangles back to back. Their shorter sides are about three hands, their longest between five and six hands.

I think of that figure as *two* triangles rather than one with one extra star. That makes the Siamese twin figure more easily recognized when one twin is below the horizon.

Naming the stars, as if they were all in one triangle, clockwise you have:

Regulus	(REG-gyou-luhs)
Spica	(SPEYE-kuh)
Antares	(an-TAYR-eez) and
Arcturus	(ark-TOO-ruhs)

To remember these names, in the order given, I think of the cook on the ship with the polished rigging. He is making soup for the impossible captain and laces it with:

REGular SPices ANd ARsenic

That reminds me of Regulus, Spica, Antares, and Arcturus.

THE TRIANGLE: Near the 20^h line and entirely north of the celestial equator I see a triangle, each side of which measures about three hands. Again clockwise, the stars are named:

Vega	(VEE-guh)
Altair	(al-TAYR) and
Deneb	(DEN-eb)

To remember the names, I think of the cook's trial. The prosecutor proposes to show that the cook poisoned the captain's vegetables. The cook denies it. (After all, it was the soup!) The newspaper headlines the story:

VEGetable ALTeration DENied

That reminds me of Vega, Altair, and Deneb.

ONE STAR: Fomalhaut (FOH-muhl-ot) is left over. (According to different sources, the last syllable is also pronounced *-hoh, -oh,* or *-oht.*) It is near the 23^h line, so it will be south of you and highest in the sky when star time is 23^h. It is in declination 30°S, so it will be three hands below the high point that you used to trace the celestial equator. In

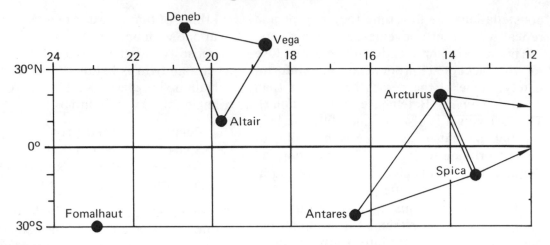

Fig. 11. Star map for star time 6–18ʰ. Twelve of the fifteen first-magnitude stars visible everywhere in the coverage area are within 30° (three hands) of the celestial equator. The remaining three are within a little more than 40° (two spans) from that line.

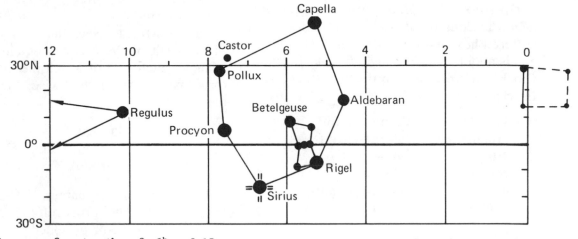

Fig. 12. Star map for star time 0–6ʰ and 18–24ʰ.

latitude 40°N, that point will have been five hands above your southern horizon. Fomalhaut then will be two hands above your horizon and due south.

I'll give you another clue for finding that star presently.

You will recall that this star map, like the corresponding map of the world, is not a strip with two ends but a ring. To show the ring on paper, I have slit it open at the 0ʰ

line. You should have no trouble matching the resulting strip with the sky when your star time is between 6ʰ and 18ʰ.

But look what happens when the star time at your location is, say, 2ʰ. The stars to the left of the 2ʰ line are on the right page, the ones to the right on the left page. Very awkward.

The next figure shows the ring split along the 12ʰ line and will keep everything together

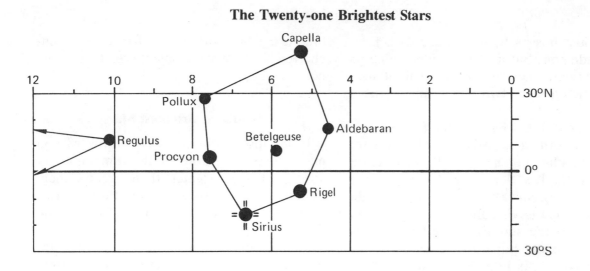

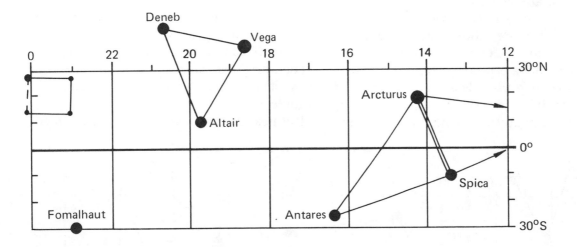

when it would be awkward with the first star map.

In redrawing the basic strip, I have made a few additions.

Inside the hexagon I have added the brighter stars of the constellation Orion (oh-REYE-uhn). That's one constellation many readers will already know. It contains two first-magnitude stars: Betelgeuse, the star in the center of the hexagon, and Rigel.

Note that the three central stars—the Belt of Orion—are virtually on the celestial equator. That means whenever Orion is visible, you'll have a check on your tracing of that line. It must go right through the belt. By the way, continuing the line of the Belt toward the east leads to Sirius, the brightest of all fixed stars.

Near the hexagon I have also added the star Castor (KAS-tor), the twin of Pollux.

Castor just misses being classed as a first-magnitude star, but it helps in identifying its brighter twin. There is no other pair of such bright stars a mere two fingers apart within the strip.

Near the 0^h line I have added four dimmer stars that form a slightly lopsided square, more than a hand on a side. I didn't make up that pattern. It's the Great Square or the Square of Pegasus (PEG-uh-suhs). Its right (western) edge is virtually at the same right ascension as the star Fomalhaut. When the right edge of the Square of Pegasus is due south of you, so is Fomalhaut. But it will be more than two spans closer to your horizon. At all other times imagine the right edge of the Square pointing at Fomalhaut. There is no bright star anywhere near Fomalhaut, and planets never stray into its vicinity.

You'll read more about the planets in Chapters 5 and 6. For now, just one clue: The planets always stay within the main frame of the strip map, less than 30 degrees north or south of the celestial equator.

The two strips in this chapter show all the brightest stars within that frame. Any uncharted bright starlike object seen there *must* be a planet.

Southern Brightest Stars

From about latitude 34°N southward you may see one or more of the remaining six stars that are brighter than second magnitude. That line runs roughly through Los Angeles, Atlanta, Casablanca, Beirut, and Osaka.

These stars will appear low in your southern sky in the gap left between the bottom edge of the strip map, tilted for your latitude, and your southern horizon. You may imagine them hanging from the edge of the map and identify them that way.

Canopus (kuh-NOH-puhs) is the first of these stars to appear when you travel south in the Northern Hemisphere. It is the second-brightest star in the sky. Theoretically it just gets above your horizon in latitude 37°N.

But near the horizon all stars are dimmed.

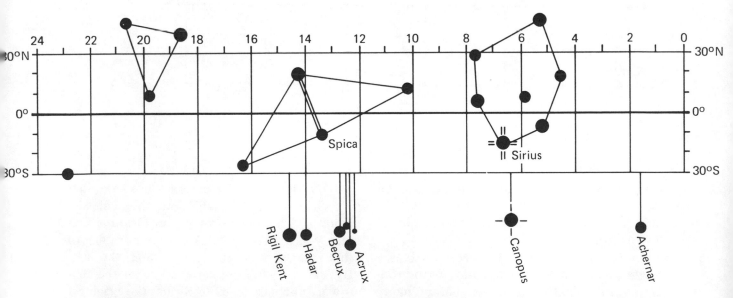

Fig. 13. Southern brightest stars. The six first-magnitude stars visible only in the southernmost part of the coverage area have been added to the basic strip map (also two dimmer ones to complete the constellation of the Southern Cross).

You are familiar with that effect: You can't look at the sun when it's high in the sky, but at rising and setting its rays, slanting through the densest, water-laden part of the atmosphere, are weakened. At these times you can watch the sun quite comfortably.

Canopus will not appear as a first-magnitude star—brighter than Castor—until you reach latitude 34°N. Finding it is easy. By coincidence, it is almost on the same hour circle as Sirius. When Sirius bears south (star time about $6\frac{1}{2}^h$) Canopus will be near your southern horizon, $3\frac{1}{2}$ hands below Sirius.

Canopus becomes impressive in southernmost Florida. There it will climb a little more than one hand above the horizon, having risen three hands east of south (star time 3^h), and setting as far west of south seven hours later.

The visibility of the other five southern first-magnitude stars remains marginal outside the Tropics. They barely rise above the horizon and lose much of their brightness by absorption in the atmosphere.

You can find four of these five by using Spica as reference star. All four happen to be at about the same distance from the celestial equator and so describe similar small arcs centered on the south point of your horizon.

About one hour *before* Spica bears south, Acrux (AY-kruhks) and Becrux (BAY-kruhks), two of the four stars that form the famed Southern Cross, will be due south of you, just above the horizon (star time $12\frac{1}{2}^h$).

STARS VISIBLE ANYWHERE IN COVERAGE AREA

Star	RA^h	Superconstellation	Notes
Aldebaran	4 1/2	Hexagon	
Altair	19 3/4	Triangle	
Antares	16 1/2	Double Triangle	
Arcturus	14 1/4	Double Triangle	
Betelgeuse	6	Hexagon	Center of hexagon
Capella	5 1/4	Hexagon	North of strip chart
Deneb	20 3/4	Triangle	North of strip chart
Fomalhaut	23	—	Find from Square of Pegasus
Pollux	7 3/4	Hexagon	Castor nearby
Procyon	7 1/2	Hexagon	
Regulus	10	Double Triangle	
Rigel	5 1/4	Hexagon	
Sirius	6 3/4	Hexagon	
Spica	13 1/2	Double Triangle	
Vega	18 1/2	Triangle	North of strip chart

STARS VISIBLE ONLY IN SOUTHERN PART OF COVERAGE AREA

Star	RA^h	Find from	Notes
Achernar	1 1/2		South 2½^h after Fomalhaut
Acrux	12 1/2	Spica	
Becrux	12 3/4	Spica	
Canopus	6 1/2	Sirius	
Hadar	14	Spica	
Rigil Kent	14 1/2	Spica	

Fig. 14. The twenty-one brightest (first-magnitude) stars. *RA* indicates star time when a star is due south of you, and highest in the sky.

About one hour *after* Spica bears south, Hadar (HA-dar) and Rigil Kent (REYE-juhl KENT) will pass—in that order—south of you (star time 14½ʰ).

Rigil Kent, also known as Alpha Centauri (AL-fuh sen-TOH-ree) is one of the very nearest stars. Hadar is perhaps better known as Beta Centauri (BAY-tuh sen-TOH-ree).

In southernmost Florida, when Spica bears south of you (star time 13½ʰ) all four of these stars, in the order I have mentioned them, from west to east, will be low above your southern horizon (Acrux a little lower than the other three).

That leaves only one southern first-magnitude star: Achernar (AY-ker-nar). I can give you little help in finding it, except that it will be south of you when your star time is 1½ʰ. It will appear at that time about a finger higher than the stars south of Spica when they are at their highest.

3

Constellations from the Brightest Stars

Everybody knows what a constellation is: a pattern of stars. If I pressed you for a more accurate definition, you might add: a pattern of stars easily seen with the naked eye. But even that does not describe what we usually call a constellation: a widely accepted pattern.

Most of the constellations you have ever heard of go back to the astronomer Ptolemy's catalog of about A.D. 140. He listed forty-eight constellations mainly named after gods, heroes, and animals. Stars left out of these traditional constellations were quaintly called "unformed" stars. A few more constellations were later constructed from these stars.

Ptolemy observed the stars in Alexandria, latitude 31°N. So he didn't include a vast area of the sky that becomes visible only when you watch the sky in the Tropics and the Southern Hemisphere. In all, forty constellations were added to the official list since Ptolemy, giving a total of eighty-eight recognized constellations.

The stars, contrary to appearance, are not glued to the celestial sphere. Some are near—by astronomical standards; some, far away. The stars in any one constellation may not have any more to do with one another than the moon and the tree behind which it seems to rise. Move a few steps to one side, and the moon rises behind another tree. Travel out into deep space, and you'd see totally different patterns.

You might then be tempted to define a constellation as an accepted pattern of stars as seen from Earth. Even that definition is not satisfactory. It includes *asterisms*.

You have already encountered two such asterisms. The Square of Pegasus is formed by stars belonging to two separate constellations, Pegasus and Andromeda (an-DROM-uh-duh). The Belt of Orion is a group of three stars in the constellation Orion.

Asterism (from Greek *aster,* "star") and *constellation* (from Latin *stella,* "star") once meant the same thing. Some modern dictionaries define an asterism as a *small* grouping of stars. That's fine for the Belt of Orion and several other asterisms. But it won't do, for instance, for the Summer Triangle (our superconstellation Triangle), three hands on a side.

Asterisms and constellations were invented as memory aids for stargazers. For the modern, casual stargazer they are not much help.

They are not easy to learn and remember. Most of them don't look like the people, animals, and things after which they are named. The moon, a streetlamp, and the sky glow from a nearby town blot out the dimmer stars that make up most of the constellations. And how could you find, say, Canis Minor (KAY-nis MEYE-nuhr), the Little Dog, where even Ptolemy could see only *two* stars?

Here is a problem: How would you recognize this pattern of stars that appears in a certain part of the sky; one of the stars is very bright, all the others rather dim—technically of third and fourth magnitude?

Fig. 16. Fanciful constellation.

dome. But that's little help when you look at the sky.

A more modern approach, found on many star finders, is to connect some of the stars with straight lines. Unfortunately, the resulting figure resembles a lobster, or perhaps a slug—a snail without a shell.

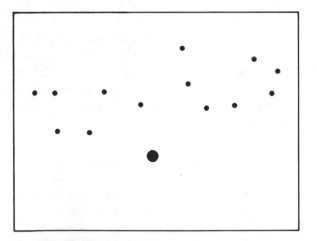

Fig. 15. Fourteen stars.

In Western tradition these stars form the constellation Virgo (VUHR-goh), the Virgin. For centuries the stars were shown sprinkled over the dress and hair of a lady. In a planetarium you may still see the female figure superimposed on the stars on the

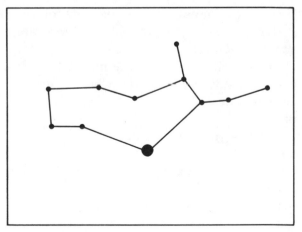

Fig. 17. Geometric pattern.

In 1952 Mr. H. A. Rey, with great imagination, redrew the outlines of the constellations to make the geometric figures look more like twins, a lion, even a girl.

For the serious stargazer Mr. Rey's figures are a great help. But to achieve his effect he had to include some stars you'll see only in a completely dark sky. And when the

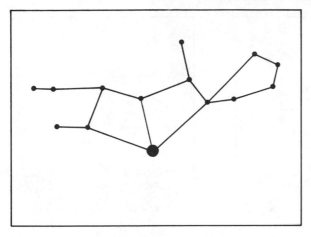

Fig. 18. H. A. Rey's figure.

sky is that dark the nonexpert may be over-whelmed by the sheer multitude of stars.

Professional astronomers to this day use the constellations. But they ignore the pattern of stars and concentrate on their territories. The boundaries of the official eighty-eight constellations were agreed upon at an international conference and are shown on star maps and star atlases.

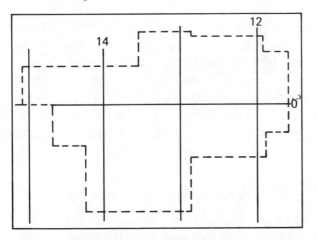

Fig. 19. Astronomer's constellation.

Told only that a comet had been spotted in Virgo, an astronomer with such a map would know exactly what area of the sky to sweep with his telescope.

For the naked-eye stargazer I suggest an-

other approach. Learn to identify the brightest stars first. (You can use full-moon nights for that. They help by blotting out all but the brightest and very bright stars.) Then from the brightest stars find some of the most prominent constellations. Later you can fill in the gaps with less bright stars and their constellations.

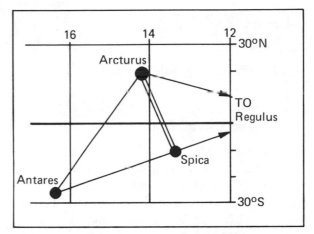

Fig. 20. Finding constellations from a bright star. *Example :* **Virgo (the Virgin) from Spica.**

Connecting constellation outlines, even after you have found their brightest star, is still a challenge. One problem: The constellations don't always appear upright or near upright. Look how, for instance, the Lion changes (Fig. 21).

And south of the equator you'll find all your old northern friends standing on their heads.

Figure 22 will introduce you to the fourteen constellations you can find from the fifteen brightest stars visible everywhere in the area covered by this part of the book.

I'll talk about them in the order in which you met the stars in the preceding chapter. I'll also give you some details about the strange star names. Some of them help in connecting stars and constellations. Many of the odd star names come to us from Ptolemy in Arabic translation.

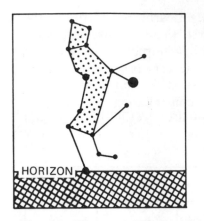

Fig. 21. The constellation Leo (the Lion).

Constellations from the Hexagon

Betelgeuse, the star in the center of the hexagon, is, as you already know, in the constellation Orion (oh-REYE-uhn). In Arabic, its name means "shoulder." That's where it is in Mr. Rey's drawing.

Capella (Latin, meaning "little she-goat") is in the constellation Auriga (o-REYE-guh), the Charioteer. Did he use goats to pull his chariot? Unlikely. But the image of one little she-goat pulling a chariot may help you connect Capella and Auriga.

Aldebaran (Arabic, "the follower") is in the constellation Taurus (TO-ruhs), the Bull. There it follows the Pleiades (PLEE-uh-deez), or Seven Sisters, another asterism (the black rectangle in Fig. 42). If your eyes are quite exceptionally good you may see up to six closely packed dim stars in that asterism. More likely you'll see a bright little cloud with some brighter spots.

Rigel (Arabic for "foot") is also in the constellation Orion. (That explains why from fifteen stars we can locate only fourteen constellations.) It's one of Orion's feet, diagonally opposite Betelgeuse, and on your right. Perhaps *right* will help you remember Rigel.

Sirius, sometimes called the Dog Star, is in Canis Major (KAY-nis MAY-jer), the Big Dog. The word Sirius—latinized Greek—means

"scorcher." English has the same root in the word *sear*. For a memory aid you could try: Searing days, dog days, the Dog Star in the Big Dog.

Procyon (Greek, meaning "before the dog") is in Canis Minor (KAY-nis MEYE-nuhr), the Little Dog, the constellation containing just two stars. Procyon got its name from rising, say, in Athens (latitude 38°N) before the dog star. But not far south of that latitude, Sirius rises first.

Pollux is in Gemini (JEM-i-neye or JEM-i-nee), the Twins. There's no doubt about the name Pollux. It's from Greek mythology: the son of Leda and Zeus, the twin of Castor. Most people would refer to these twins as Castor and Pollux. Here Pollux is the brighter boy. Interestingly, it was not always so. One of the few recorded changes in brightness has made Castor dimmer than its twin.

Constellations from the Double Triangle

Regulus (Latin for "little king," from *rex,* a full-sized king) is in the constellation Leo (LEE-oh), the Lion. For a memory aid you could try: The lion, king of beasts.

Spica is in Virgo (VUHR-goh), the Virgin, as you already know. Spica, in Latin, means "spike of grain." The connection between that and the name of the constellation is unclear. One explanation has the maiden carry an ear of corn or a sheaf of wheat—a young goddess of fertility. For a memory aid, you might try this: Sacrifice a spike of corn in place of a virgin.

Antares is in Scorpius (SKOR-pi-uhs), formerly Scorpio, the Scorpion. There's no argument about the meaning of the star's name. It means the rival of Ares, the Greek war god, the planet we usually call by its Latin name, Mars. The rivalry—apart from mythology—is in their reddish color.

Scorpius is one of the few constellations that resemble their namesakes. It takes only a little imagination to see in its brighter stars a scorpion complete with stinger at the tail. Antares is at the head of the critter, just behind the pincers.

For southern stargazers, Scorpius is a useful constellation for quickly orienting oneself in the sky. It is almost always visible when Orion is below the horizon. Already in latitude 35°N it rises within one hour of Orion's setting and sets less than two hours before Orion rises. The periods when neither constellation is visible get shorter as you go farther south.

There, if you just learn to recognize these two constellations, you'll have a friend in the sky almost all the time. Either constellation lets you quickly align the strip map of the brightest stars without bothering with local star time.

Arcturus is in Boötes (bo-OH-tees), the Bear Driver, also called the Herdsman. Arcturus—Latinized Greek—also means "bear driver" (you may recognize the root of *ursa* in it). It is also translated as "bear guard." Memory aid: It does indeed drive—or guard against, as a herdsman—the Big Bear, about which you'll read in the next chapter.

Constellations from the Triangle

Vega is in the constellation Lyra (LEYE-ruh), the Lyre. The translation of the star's name—from Arabic—is no help here: the "falling eagle" or "falling vulture." How does that beast get entangled in the strings of a musical instrument? Was Lyra once known as the Falling Eagle, to distinguish it from the next constellation?

Altair is in Aquila (AK-wi-luh), the Eagle. Altair means either "flying eagle" or "flying vulture" according to different sources. A possible memory aid: The eagle flies at great altitudes. Altair, by the way, has two nearby stars that make positively identifying it easy if the sky is not too bright. Both are about a finger's width away; the northern one is brighter than the southern one.

Deneb is in Cygnus (SIG-nuhs), the Swan. The Arabic word translates, I'm told, into "tail of the hen." So this swan has a hen's tail. Don't let the sketch mislead you: Deneb is in the tail; the long line is the bird's outstretched neck. The Swan flies southeast, trying to pass between Lyra and Aquila, which is headed in the opposite direction.

(There is more confusion to be avoided: There is a star with a similar name, Denebola (de-NEB-oh-luh), which in Arabic means "the tail of the lion." That's exactly where you find it: the star numbered 28 in Leo.)

The Northern Cross, one more asterism, is formed by the five brightest stars in Cygnus. A line from Deneb to the swan's head forms the long arm of the cross; the stars at the wing tips, the short arm. There is no danger of confusing the five-star asterism of the Northern Cross with the four stars that form the constellation Southern Cross, or Crux (KRUHKS). One is well north of the basic strip map, about four hands north of the equator. The other is six hands south of that line.

Fomalhaut

The star left out of the superconstellations, Formalhaut, is in Piscis Austrinus (PIS-is OS-TREYE-nuhs), the Southern Fish, an incon-

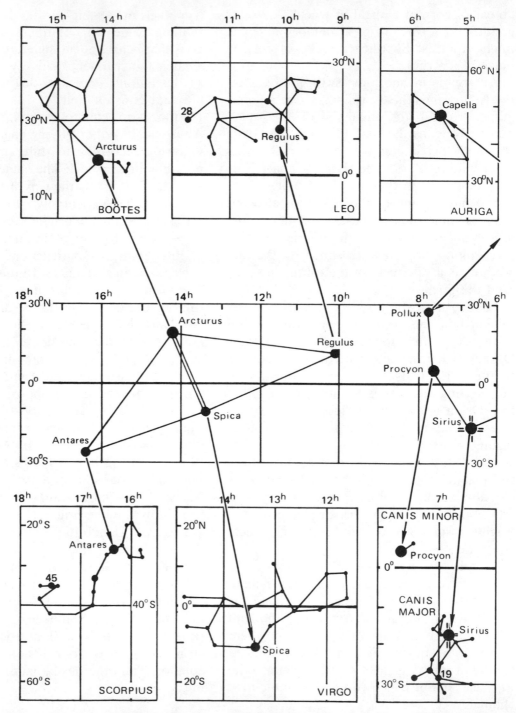

Fig. 22. Finding constellations from the fifteen brightest stars that are visible everywhere in the coverage area. All constellations—Mr. Rey's outlines—are shown bearing south and are slightly enlarged from the strip map. The 10° marks and the hour lines (1ʰ = 15°) let you measure distances in and between constellations (one hand = 10°). The small numerals refer to navigational stars, listed in Fig. 44.

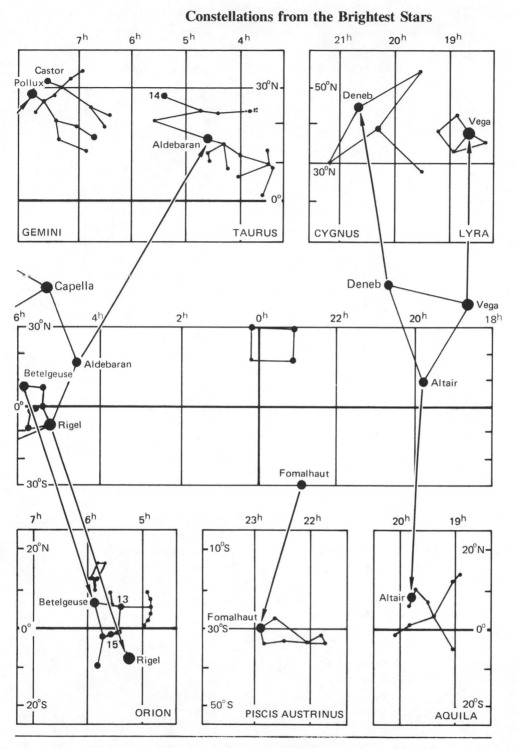

GEMINI

Castor
Pollux

14

Aldebaran

TAURUS

CYGNUS

Deneb

Vega

LYRA

Capella

Deneb

Vega

Betelgeuse

Aldebaran

Altair

Rigel

Fomalhaut

Betelgeuse

13

15

Rigel

ORION

Fomalhaut

PISCIS AUSTRINUS

Altair

AQUILA

R

Star name	Constellation (Latin)	Constellation (English)
Achernar	Eridanus	River
Acrux	Crux	Southern Cross
Aldebaran	Taurus	Bull
Altair	Aquila	Eagle
Antares	Scorpius	Scorpion
Arcturus	Boötes	Bear Driver
Becrux (Mimosa)	Crux	Southern Cross
Betelgeuse	Orion	Orion
Canopus	Carina	Keel
Capella	Auriga	Charioteer
Deneb	Cygnus	Swan
Fomalhaut	Piscis Austrinus	Southern Fish
Hadar	Centaurus	Centaur
Pollux	Gemini	Twins
Procyon	Canis Minor	Little Dog
Regulus	Leo	Lion
Rigel	Orion	Orion
Rigil Kent	Centaurus	Centaur
Sirius	Canis Major	Big Dog
Spica	Virgo	Virgin
Vega	Lyra	Lyre

Constellation (Latin)	Constellation (English)	First-mag. Star(s)
Aquila	Eagle	Altair
Auriga	Charioteer	Capella
Boötes	Bear Driver	Arcturus
Canis Major	Big Dog	Sirius
Canis Minor	Little Dog	Procyon
Carina	Keel	Canopus
Centaurus	Centaur	Rigil Kent, Hadar
Crux	Southern Cross	Acrux, Becrux (Mimosa)
Cygnus	Swan	Deneb
Eridanus	River	Achernar
Gemini	Twins	Pollux
Leo	Lion	Regulus
Lyra	Lyre	Vega
Orion	Orion	Betelgeuse, Rigel
Piscis Austrinus	Southern Fish	Fomalhaut
Scorpius	Scorpion	Antares
Taurus	Bull	Aldebaran
Virgo	Virgin	Spica

Fig. 23. First-magnitude stars and their constellations. Use the top part to get the name of a constellation from a known star. Use the bottom part to get the reference star for a given constellation.

spicuous constellation. Don't be disappointed if you can't see it.

This constellation should not be confused with Pisces (PIS-eez or PEYE-suhs), the Fishes—note the plural—a constellation in the zodiac (see Chapter 7).

Even if you are far enough south to glimpse occasionally the remaining six first-magnitude stars, there is only one constellation they'll help you find: Crux (KRUHKS), the Southern Cross.

4

The Northernmost Stars and Constellations

You started the study of the sky by imagining a strip map aligned with the night sky where and when you watch it. That meant placing the equator on the map over the celestial equator at your latitude. It also meant bringing the hour line corresponding to your star time to bear south of you.

For observers south of about latitude 35°N I added six very bright stars that will at times appear between the bottom of the strip map and their southern horizon. That space is labeled SOUTHERN GAP in the next illustration.

Even with that—and the addition of three bright stars outside the basic strip (Capella, Vega, and Deneb)—I have left a part of the sky uncovered. It is your northern sky. On a globe of the world it would be the area around the North Pole. In the sky it is the area around the *celestial* North Pole, the area labeled POLAR CAP in the next figure.

So far we have used a map that resembles

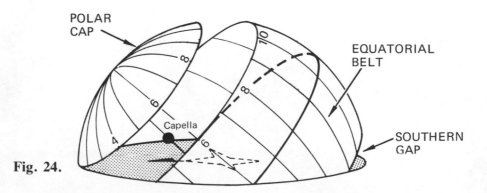

POLAR CAP

EQUATORIAL BELT

SOUTHERN GAP

Capella

Fig. 24.

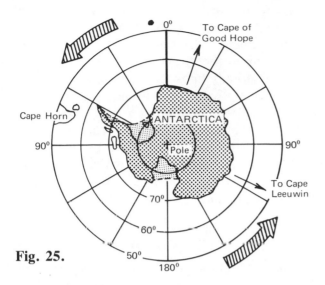

Fig. 25.

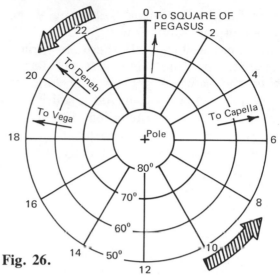

Fig. 26.

a map of the world not too far from the equator. To cover the polar cap, you'll use a different sky map.

Every atlas has a map of Antarctica, the continent around the South Pole.

The pole is in the center of the map, surrounded by circles that represent the parallels of latitude. The longitude lines (meridians) radiate from the pole like the spokes of a wheel. The zero longitude line, the meridian of Greenwich, is shown as a heavier line in this sketch.

Such a map of Antarctica may include the southern tip of South America to help you orient yourself. But on most maps Africa and Australia are too far away to be shown. Here arrows point to well-known points on these continents.

The map you'll be using for the northern polar cap is constructed on similar lines.

The celestial North Pole is in the center, surrounded by circles of declination. The hour lines radiate from the pole like the spokes of a wheel. The zero hour line is shown as a heavier line.

We can again use arrows to point to features—stars, constellations or asterisms—too far from the pole to be included in the map, just as on the map of Antarctica.

Aligning the Polar Star Chart

Matching the polar star map to the night sky is not difficult.

First you find the celestial North Pole. For that you have three clues.

ONE: It is exactly north of you.

TWO: It is as many degrees above your northern horizon as you are north of the equator. In latitude 40°N, that makes 40 degrees—two spans.

THREE: The polestar, Polaris, is now within half a finger's width of the celestial North Pole.

All this works in reverse. Find Polaris and you have located the celestial North Pole. And you have found north. Measure the distance between your horizon and Polaris with your hand, and you have found your latitude close enough to trace the celestial equator.

Polaris is a bright (second-magnitude) star that remains clearly visible on a full-moon night. If you know approximate north, look for it by measuring your approximate latitude upward from the north horizon. No great precision is needed in either direction or latitude. There's no star bright enough to be confused with Polaris within more than one and a half hands from it.

Most people in the Northern Hemisphere recognize the Big Dipper—seven stars of about the same brightness that form the shape of a dipper, or, if you are British, a plow. It's not a constellation, but another asterism—part of the constellation Ursa Major (UHR-suh MAY-jer), the Big Bear.

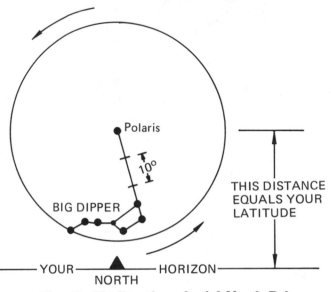

Fig. 27. Finding the celestial North Pole.

The two stars that form the side of the dipper that's away from the handle almost point to Polaris. Hence their name: Pointers; they make up another asterism. They are about 5½ degrees—less than three fingers—apart. Polaris (of about the same brightness) is five times that distance—not quite three hands—from the nearer Pointer.

The Big Dipper will not always appear below the polestar as it does in the drawing. Six hours after it was in the position shown, it will appear standing on its handle, to the east (right) of Polaris. Another six hours later, it will be emptying its contents on Polaris. Another six hours later, if it were still dark, you'd see it hanging by its handle, to the west (left) of Polaris. About twenty-four hours after the first observation it will be back at the position of the night before, below Polaris. (To see the effect, just turn the book in the direction of the arrows.)

You already know that for "about twenty-four hours" you should read 23^{h}56^m. That's the time it takes Earth to turn once on its axis, the imaginary line that runs from the North to the South Pole, like the shaft of a globe. It is that rotation which makes all the stars here seem to go around—counterclockwise—the celestial North Pole.

Two More Constellations

About eight fingers from Polaris, in the direction of the outermost star in the handle of the Big Dipper, is a star of about the same magnitude as Polaris: Kochab (KOH-kab).

Kochab, Polaris, and five dimmer stars form another dipper-shaped pattern. (Kochab is in the same position as the Pointer nearest Polaris in the Big Dipper.) That's the constellation Ursa Minor (UHR-suh MEYE-nuhr), the Little Bear. It's hard to see unless conditions are good. When they are you won't have any trouble tracing its pattern.

On the other side of Polaris, away from Kochab and the Big Dipper, is a bright constellation: Cassiopeia (kass-i-oh-PEE-uh). It is supposed to look like the queen of that name sitting in a chair. You may see five stars—about as bright as Polaris—forming a chair, right side up, sideways, or upside down. You may see the same five stars as a sloppy letter *M* when they are above Polaris, as a *W* when they are below.

North of about latitude 40°N, Cassiopeia and the Big Dipper will be above your horizon at all hours of every night.

But the height of the celestial North Pole above your horizon depends, as you know, on your latitude. It will sink lower as you move south. There must be a point where, say, the Big Dipper will begin to sink partially below your horizon when it's below

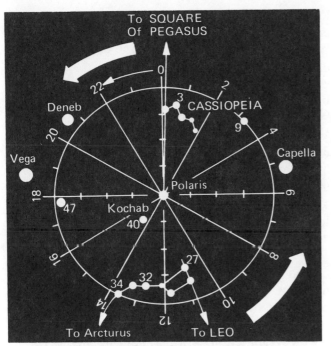

Fig. 28. Map of northernmost stars.

great effort. So you may want to work the problem in reverse:

> To get star time for aligning the strip map, match the appearance of the Big Dipper, Cassiopeia, and Polaris in the sky by turning the book. Whatever numeral is now on top is your star time.

Example: To match the sky some night you had to turn the book until the top was between 5 and 6, but nearer 5. Call it 5¼ if you like. Now align your strip map for that star time. Capella will be directly above the south point of your horizon, high in the sky, near your zenith.

In this example Capella happens to be on both the polar star map and the strip map. Vega and Deneb are also on both maps. You could use any of these three stars to prove that the star time found by this method gives the correct alignment for star time to your strip map.

Here is an *alternate method* for finding star time from the northern sky. Find Polaris and Kochab, the star about as bright as Polaris and about eight fingers distant (toward the handle of the Big Dipper, or away from Cassiopeia).

Consider the line from Polaris to Kochab the hour hand of a clock. Read the star time from the dial shown in Figure 29. If the stars happen to be in the position shown, you'd read star time 5ʰ, without even having to turn the book. There is no danger of your mistaking another star for Kochab: There is none

Polaris. The star at the end of the handle, being the farthest from the pole, will be the first to disappear. When you reach the latitude of central Florida, the entire dipper will be below your horizon when it's directly below Polaris.

Cassiopeia, being on the opposite side of the polestar, will then be high in your northern sky as a lazy *M*. It will help you spot Polaris, less than three hands away.

Star Time and the Northern Sky

You could get the relative position of Cassiopeia and the Big Dipper before even looking at the sky. You could turn Figure 28 so that your star time of the moment is uppermost. That's the same star time you used to align the strip map. You can see that this is so in Figure 24.

You could get the star time from the table. But learning to recognize the Big Dipper, Cassiopeia, and Polaris—in whatever position—is easy. Turning the book is no

Fig. 29.

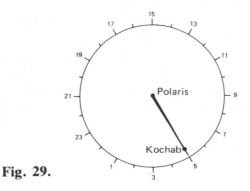

anywhere near it, and no planet ever gets into this area.

Both methods for finding star time from the northern sky have two advantages over finding approximate star time from standard time and a table. You don't have to allow for Daylight Saving Time. And it does not matter where in your time zone you look at the sky.

That makes these methods more accurate than the table.

(In theory, your *local* time, the time that matters here, could differ by plus or minus ½ hour from standard time, the time shown by your clock unless it happens to be on Daylight Saving Time. To keep a whole state, province, or country on the same standard time, the half-hour limit is sometimes stretched. *Example:* In El Paso, Texas, star time calculated from Central Standard Time would be well over one hour slow on star time read from the sky.)

The Northern Sky and the Strip Map

The northern sky not only gives you accurate star time, free of man-made complications such as daylight time and zone time. It also gives you true south, free from any error of the compass: directly opposite the bearing of Polaris.

Unless your northern horizon is obstructed—say, by high mountains—it also gives you the latitude you need to align the strip map.

Example: You measure the height of Polaris above your northern horizon as three hands (30 degrees) and three fingers (6 degrees). Your latitude then is very close to 36°N.

You could measure that same distance down from your zenith, three hands and three fingers, to get the high point of the ce-

lestial equator. Standing or sitting, it is not easy to locate the zenith accurately. Even lying down, you could be several degrees off in your estimate.

The better way—unless high mountains block your southern horizon—is to measure 90 degrees minus your latitude up from the southern horizon. In the example (latitude 36°N) you'd measure 54 degrees—five hands and two fingers—upward to find the point to salute while facing due south. You then swing your arm east, back through the point found, and west to trace the celestial equator.

You will discover for yourself some connections between the stars shown on the polar star map and those on the strip chart.

The Big Dipper is a good starting point.

One connection, with a built-in memory aid, is this: Follow the *arc* of the dipper handle and you'll land on Arcturus. *Speed* on in the same direction and you'll hit Spica. (That memory aid was obviously invented by someone who used the variant pronunciation SPEE-kuh.)

Or continue the line from the Pointers through Polaris and you'll get to the western edge of the Square of Pegasus, three spans from Polaris.

As the Pointers lead to Polaris, so the two stars at the handle side of the Big Dipper point to Vega, three spans away. In the opposite direction they and the Pointers lead roughly to Regulus, about five hands distant, and certainly to the constellation Leo.

You may never bother with any of these connections. With just the polar star map and the strip map you can find your way around the night sky very well. You already know all the brightest stars and more than a score of constellations and asterisms.

It's time we looked at the planets.

5

Magnitude of Stars and Planets

Up until now I have used the term *magnitude* a few times, explaining only that it was a measure of brightness of stars. You took it for granted that second-magnitude stars were dimmer than first-magnitude stars.

You were not surprised to find the symbols on our star maps more prominent for brighter stars. You were used to that from other maps that show villages, towns, and cities with increasingly prominent symbols.

Even if I had not mentioned it, you would have understood that magnitude is measured here, on Earth. This apparent magnitude says nothing about the size of a star or the brightness of its surface. Stars vary greatly in both respects. Magnitude is simply a measure of brightness as seen at the distance the star happens to be from us.

We now know that our sun is a very average star in both size and surface brightness. But it is so close to us that it has taken astronomers several thousand years to realize that it is simply a star—or, to put it differently, that the stars we see are suns.

The very earliest Western star catalogs—those of Hipparchus (ca. 150 B.C.) and Ptolemy, about three hundred years later—grouped the fixed stars in six classes of brightness. Much as a child spending a summer at the seashore might store shells, by size, in six boxes. The first box would contain the largest shells; the second, smaller ones; and so on. You'd have to strain to see the individual shells in the last box.

The early astronomers' first box held all the brightest stars, down to the present brightness of Castor. The second held Polaris and most of the stars of the Big Dipper and Cassiopeia, among others. You'd have to strain, under the best conditions, to see individual stars in the last box.

The catalogs listed more than one thousand stars. It must have taken a great deal of patience to classify their magnitude. The method employed is still used today for certain astronomical tasks: comparing one star with some neighboring stars. We now have more objective methods: measuring photographic images of the stars, or converting the light of a star into electricity and measuring the current. Results are given to one or two decimals of one magnitude.

The modern magnitude scale is directly comparable with the ancient scheme. Any star that measures between magnitude 1.5 and 2.5 (or 1.50 and 2.49) is a second-magnitude star; a star between 2.50 and 3.49 is a third-magnitude star; and so forth.

But there are differences.

Traditionally, all stars brighter than second magnitude were classified as first-magnitude stars. That's fair enough for conversation. But how do you assign numbers and decimals to the brightest fixed stars and the planets that often outshine the brightest stars?

The solution is simple: After magnitude one comes magnitude zero, then minus one, minus two. . . . You have used the same idea talking about temperature. When the temperature drops from one degree above zero (+1° Fahrenheit or Celsius) you read 0°, then −1°, −2°, and so on.

Castor is listed as magnitude +1.6; that

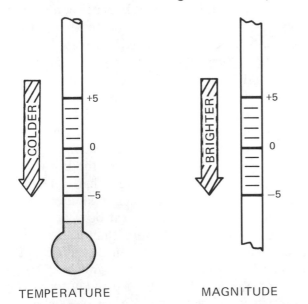

TEMPERATURE   MAGNITUDE

Fig. 30. Minus magnitude and minus temperatures.

makes it a second-magnitude star. Its brighter twin, Pollux, is +1.2; Altair, a little brighter than Pollux, rates +0.9; Vega is close to magnitude zero (+0.1). Only two stars have minus magnitudes: Canopus (−0.9) and Sirius (−1.6).

So whenever you talk about magnitudes of stars everyone will know you mean plus magnitudes; just as everyone understands when you complain about the heat that you mean +100°F. or +38°C.

At first, minus numbers—you'll meet many more when you read about the planets—seem needlessly confusing. Why not start the scale at the brightest planet to get rid of minus numbers? But that would make first-magnitude (Procyon (+0.5) a fifth-magnitude star—even more confusing!

Other scales have been proposed, but the one just outlined is the one in universal use on star finders, star atlases, etc.

With the naked eye under good conditions you'll see stars down to the fifth magnitude. The scale does not stop there. In your own telescope you may see stars as faint as eleventh magnitude. The Mount Palomar telescope brings in stars down to twenty-fourth magnitude.

The magnitudes given are always understood to apply to the star or planet when it is directly overhead, at your zenith, where its light is least diminished by the atmosphere.

Halfway up the sky—four or five hands above your horizon—the difference between zenith magnitude and observed magnitude is a negligible 0.1 magnitude.

But close to the horizon—quite apart from haze—all stars and planets are dimmed. Their light there has a longer path through the absorbing atmosphere; that's also what dims (and reddens) the rising and setting sun. The technical term for that phenomenon is *atmospheric extinction.*

One span above the horizon, a star or planet loses one half magnitude. One hand above the horizon, it loses one whole mag-

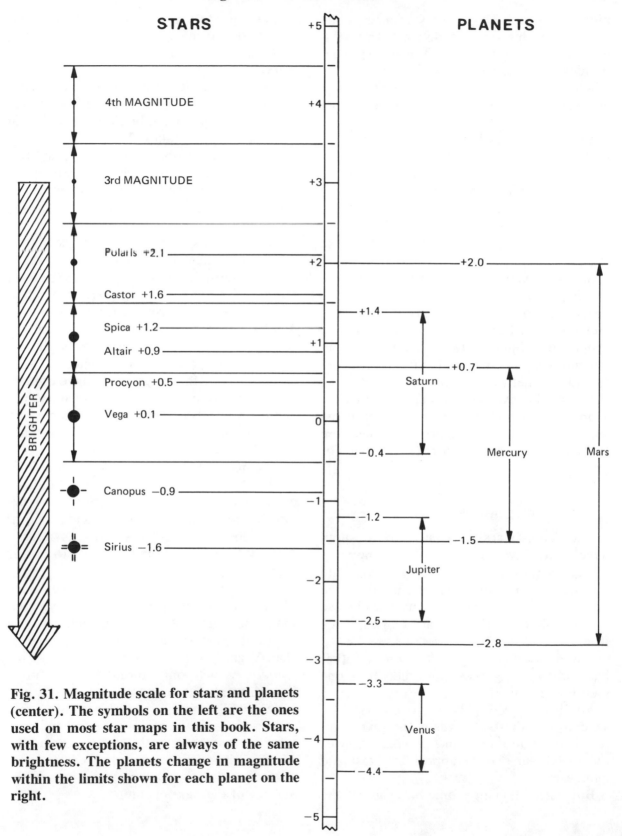

Fig. 31. Magnitude scale for stars and planets (center). The symbols on the left are the ones used on most star maps in this book. Stars, with few exceptions, are always of the same brightness. The planets change in magnitude within the limits shown for each planet on the right.

nitude (a second-magnitude star appears like a higher-up third-magnitude star). Three fingers above the horizon, it loses 1½ magnitudes; two fingers above the horizon, 2 whole magnitudes (a second-magnitude star appears like a higher-up fourth-magnitude star).

The magnitudes here discussed are *visual* magnitudes: i.e., seen by the human eye. Our vision is keenest in the yellow part of the spectrum and falls off toward both the red and blue ends. The stars are not all of the same hue. Betelgeuse, for example, is distinctly reddish compared to nearby bluish Rigel.

Modern magnitudes, measured by photographic plates or electronic devices, differ according to the color sensitivity of the method used. But they can be converted to visual magnitudes. The slightly different magnitudes you may find in different lists are due to the method of conversion.

Where the eye sees a single star a telescope often reveals two (or more) closely associated stars. All the figures given here are the *combined* magnitudes of the pair or group.

Magnitudes of Planets

The fixed stars you have read about have—with few exceptions—the same magnitude as they had in Ptolemy's day. And they have—with some exceptions—the same magnitude year in and year out. (Betelgeuse is a notable exception; it varies on our scale from +0.1 to +1.2.)

The five naked-eye planets, on the other hand, change brightness noticeably from one month to the next.

You'll read about the reasons—there are several—for these changes in the next chapter. There you'll also find at what intervals the individual planets appear brightest and dimmest.

But just knowing something about the planets' greatest and least magnitude—their magnitude range—often helps in identifying them and distinguishing them from fixed stars.

Look at the right-hand bottom of Figure 31. You'll see that the magnitude of *Venus* varies between −4.4 at brightest and −3.3 at dimmest. That makes Venus by far the brightest starlike object in the sky, and this is always enough to identify Venus positively. It will be the first "star" to appear in the evening or the last to fade in the morning.

Jupiter at its brightest is of magnitude −2.5; at its dimmest, −1.2. That makes it most of the time brighter than the brightest fixed star, Sirius (−1.6), and always brighter than the second-brightest, Canopus (−0.9). Jupiter never gets within several hands of either of these stars. So again its brightness alone may serve to identify Jupiter.

Mars has by far the greatest range of magnitude of any planet. At times it outshines Jupiter at its brightest; at other times it's barely brighter than Polaris. But at all times Mars has a distinct reddish color.

You may not see much difference in color in the stars. When Orion is below the horizon, depriving you of the comparison between (reddish) Betelgeuse and (bluish) Rigel, look for Antares (red as Mars). Nearby Spica and Arcturus are both on the bluish side.

Saturn, the last of the four easily seen planets, is always brighter than a second-magnitude star. At least magnitude it is +1.4, at greatest magnitude −0.4, brighter than Vega.

Mercury will only rarely appear bright enough to attract your attention. When it is visible at all—for a few days or at most a few weeks—it is always close to the horizon, where atmospheric extinction makes a joke of zenith magnitude figures.

How to *find* the naked-eye planets is the subject of the next chapter.

6

The Planets

Most people are more interested in the planets than in fixed stars. I can prove that. At the planetarium, visitors and telephone callers would ask me, ''What's that star I see now in the west at about . . . ?'' At least nine times out of ten it turned out to be not a star but a planet.

That's understandable. The brightest objects draw the most attention.

There are other reasons, I think. Stars are very distant fiery balls of gas—not easy to get personally excited about. Planets are near. And they are brothers and sisters of our own Earth.

Unmanned spacecraft have flown past, measured, and photographed some planets—even landed. On Mars, space probes have scooped up samples of soil and analyzed it right on the spot, and have looked for traces of organic compounds. All that gets the planets in the news.

A *manned* flight to Mars is technically possible now. A round trip to that planet might take a couple of years. With the same technology, a space probe would take more than one hundred thousand years to reach the nearest star.

Here's another reason why planets draw attention: People who get a chance to look through a telescope at a fixed star are usually disappointed; it's still only a pinpoint of light. The planets—through even a small telescope—are something else. You see the sickle shape of Venus, the red spot and the polar flattening of Jupiter, the rings of Saturn. . . .

You probably know that there are *nine* major planets known. Astronomers also keep track of more than one thousand *minor* planets, bodies that range in size from a few hundred miles (or kilometers) down to the limit of telescopic visibility. Most of the minor planets—or planetoids, or asteroids—orbit the sun between Mars and Jupiter.

Charles Kowal of the California Institute of Technology, the discoverer of several comets and at least one more moon of Jupiter, on a plate exposed in 1977 at Mount Palomar found an object about as large as the largest asteroids, but much farther from the sun than most, between the orbits of Saturn and Uranus.

Newspapers and newscasters immediately called it the tenth planet. (Some prudently added a question mark.) At the time I write this, the International Astronomical Union has not yet taken an official stand. Until it does, you are safe to assume that the object Kowal discovered is a maverick minor planet, and recognize only nine major planets.

An easy way to remember their names, in the order of increasing distance from the sun, is by the initial letters of the words in the sentence:

My Very Educated Mother
            Just Showed Us Nine Planets.

That gives you: Mercury, Venus, Earth, Mars, Jupiter, Saturn, Uranus, Neptune, and Pluto.

I don't know who made up this memory aid. But I know it was after 1930, the year of the discovery of Pluto, the outermost planet. I also know that Mother was very educated indeed. She picked one of the rare times when all nine planets are visible. She must also have had a fairly large telescope. How else could she have shown the children Pluto, which is of fourteenth magnitude? To show Pluto as a disk, rather than a starlike dot, takes a telescope of more than 20 inches (50 cm) diameter.

Here I'll talk only about the planets you can see in the sky with the naked eye. You already know the five you can see wandering against the background of fixed stars: Mercury, Venus, Mars, Jupiter, and Saturn.

The wandering has a simple explanation. The planets, including our own planet, Earth, revolve around the sun (Figure 32).

You may credit Copernicus with first having published that explanation (in 1543). Actually it had been proposed already by Aristarchus of Samos (ca. 310–230 B.C.). Kepler (in 1609 and 1619) gave us formulas that

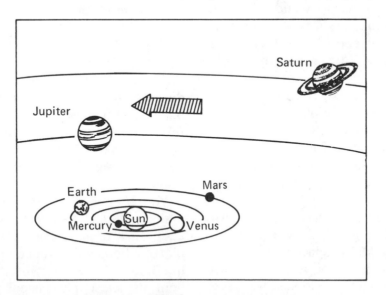

Fig. 32. The five planets visible to the naked eye and Earth—their orbits and relative size. All revolve around the sun in the direction of the arrow, and in about the same plane. To make the planets visible in the drawing—the diameter of Earth is less than one hundredth of that of the sun—they have been much enlarged (all to the same scale).

fairly well fitted the observed positions of the planets. His three "laws" were much simpler than the then generally accepted system of Ptolemy, which has sun and planets revolve around Earth. That theory required complicated geometry to make it fit observed facts.

Newton, in 1687, explained the cause of the motion of the planets—gravity—and refined Kepler's "third law," which connects the time each planet takes to circle the sun to its distance from the sun.

Perhaps you'd like some idea of these distances. Miles or kilometers are a poor measure; the figures get too large. Already for the moon, our nearest neighbor, which orbits around Earth as the planets orbit around the sun, the figure is impressive: about one quarter million statute miles (four hundred thousand kilometers).

A radio signal, which travels at the speed of light, takes a little more than one second to reach the moon, or to reach Earth from the moon. You barely noticed the delay between Houston Space Center's questions and the answers from the astronauts on the moon.

The same signal would take about three *minutes* to reach us from the nearest planet, Venus, when it's nearest Earth. From the sun it would take eight minutes. From Saturn, the farthest visible planet, it would take more than one hour. (From the nearest fixed star, light takes more than four *years* to reach us. That's about one hundred million times as long as from the moon. That's from the *nearest* star.)

Finding the Planets

To identify a bright planet that you see where no brighter star is shown on your star maps, you don't need to know any of that. And you don't need to know anything of the laws of motion.

But you may want to know in advance where among the stars you can find the planets tonight.

The astronomer, who needs to know where to point his telescope or radio dish to observe a particular planet, looks it up in an annual reference book. He doesn't, at that moment, care that in the preparation of the book the Kepler-Newton equations (with minor refinements) have been used.

For his observation he looks for the same data we have used in locating stars on our star maps and in the sky. They are: *right ascension* (the local star time when the planet will be due south) and *declination* (the planet's distance north or south of the celestial equator).

For observation of the stars—by telescope or with the naked eye—it's simplest to imagine the Earth standing still while the dome of the sky turns. In the same way, it's simplest to consider the Earth standing still while the sun and the planets move about it.

Let me start by tracing for you the path of the sun among the stars as seen from Earth. Of course, we never actually see the stars and the sun at the same time. But from the stars that disappear at sunrise, and the ones that appear at sunset, astronomers two thousand years or more ago deduced the position of the sun for any day of the year. That position is virtually the same year after year.

At the beginning of spring, about March 21, the sun is in zero declination (that is, on the celestial equator) and exactly on the zero hour line. That double zero is no coincidence. The beginning of spring is defined as the moment when the sun, northbound, crosses the equator. The zero hour line— right ascension 0^h—also by definition runs through that crossing point, the vernal equinox.

For the next six months the path of the sun will be *north* of the equator. It reaches its highest point—declination about $23\frac{1}{2}°$N—at RA 6^h around June 21. That marks the beginning of summer.

Fig. 33. The ecliptic, the apparent annual path of the sun among the stars.

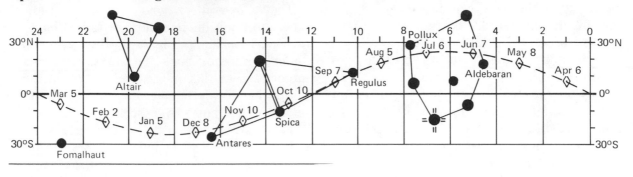

At the beginning of autumn, about September 22, the sun, now southbound, crosses the celestial equator at RA 12ʰ.

For the next six months the sun will be *south* of the celestial equator. It reaches its lowest point—declination about $23\frac{1}{2}°$S—at RA 18ʰ. That marks the beginning of winter, about December 21.

This apparent path of the sun among the stars—called the *ecliptic*—explains why, for example, Regulus is not visible on August 23, or Antares on November 30. As you can see in the diagram, the sun at these dates seems right at the place occupied by these stars.

For about ten days before and after these days, you won't be able to see these stars. They'll set or rise during twilight.

You may say you could do without that information. Nobody needs a star map to find the sun. And nobody will look for stars—or planets—until it is just about dark. Then why bring the path of the sun into this discussion of the naked-eye planets?

Simply this:

The planets will always be seen close to the line traced by the apparent motion of the sun, the ecliptic.

That explains one already stated fact: The planets will always be within the area of our basic star map, within a little more than a span from the celestial equator—never near

Deneb, Vega, or Capella; never south of the strip map; and never in the polar cap.

If the orbits of the visible planets were exactly in the Earth-sun plane, the planets would follow the ecliptic exactly. As it is, their orbits are within a few degrees of this plane. So the planets will be seen close to, but not right on, the ecliptic most of the time. The distance from the ecliptic will usually be less than a finger's width, at times increasing to less than two fingers above or below the ecliptic.

At times, that will bring the planets near five first-magnitude stars that are close to the ecliptic. They are: Aldebaran, Pollux, Regulus, Spica, and Antares. These five stars will often help you find Mars, Jupiter, and Saturn. You won't need a star to recognize superbright Venus. And no star is likely to be of much help in finding Mercury.

Besides these five stars there are two more points that help you locate the ecliptic and, from that, planets.

One is the point where the ecliptic crosses the celestial equator at 0ʰ or 24ʰ right ascension. You have known since the first chapter how to trace the celestial equator. And you'll recall that the eastern edge of the Square of Pegasus lies near the 0ʰ line. Follow that edge down to the equator and you'll have approximately located the vernal equinox.

The other point lies on a line from Altair to

Fomalhaut, not quite halfway but nearer to Fomalhaut, near the 21ʰ line.

The five stars near the ecliptic are, by coincidence, all of nearly the same magnitude (1.2). That's easy to remember. When Jupiter is near one of these stars it will always be the brighter object. Saturn occasionally and Mars for months on end could be the dimmer. You'll see later in this chapter how you can find their magnitude in any given month. It's then easy to tell which is the brighter. *Example:* You find Saturn to be near Regulus and of magnitude +0.6. Saturn will be unmistakably brighter than Regulus.

In the next few pages I'll talk about each of the naked-eye planets separately. Each has its individuality.

It would be logical to start with the innermost planet, Mercury. But I'll start with Venus, because it makes talking about Mercury easier.

Venus, with a magnitude that varies between −4.4 and −3.3, is always brighter than any star or planet—considerably brighter. It will be the first "star" to appear when it is the *Evening Star* (visible in the west at sunset), the last to disappear when it is the *Morning Star* (visible in the east at sunrise).

At the time of its greatest brightness you can see Venus in daylight without a telescope.

One way to do that is to follow it in the morning. It's clearly visible in the brightest dawn. Don't take your eyes off it. It will still be visible when the sun actually rises. Keep looking at it and you can follow it for as long as you care.

Another method works whether Venus is Morning Star or Evening Star. Take a tube such as is used for mailing calendars, or roll up a newspaper, and search where Venus should be. To avoid eye damage, don't ever look directly at the sun.

If you have seen Venus earlier in the morning sky, you'll have a fair idea where to look for it later: It will be to the right of the sun

and as many hands from the sun as it was at sunrise. It will keep nearly the same distance for several days.

If you have seen Venus the evening before, look left of the sun at the distance you remember its being from the sun at sunset. Again, it will be at nearly the same distance for several days.

The orbits of Venus and Earth are shown in Figure 34.

Their orbits and speeds of revolution around the sun combine to make Venus the Evening Star for several months. It will then disappear into the glare of the sun for a few weeks.

If the orbits of Venus and Earth were exactly in the same plane, Venus would, in the middle of this period of invisibility, pass over the face of the sun. Actually, such a *transit* of Venus is a rare event. From now until 2004 Venus will always pass just above or below the sun.

After Venus emerges from the glare of the sun it will be Morning Star for several months. Then it disappears for several months as it passes on the far side of the sun.

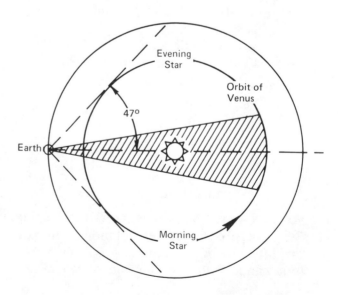

Fig. 34. Orbits of Venus and Earth seen from above.

When Venus finally emerges again as Evening Star, the cycle repeats.

When Venus becomes invisible at the *far* side of the sun it is almost six times farther from us than at its disappearance on the near side. (You can check that by measuring the drawing.) You might expect that to be the cause of its change in magnitude.

It's more complicated than that. When Venus is close to its maximum distance from us (right side of Fig. 34) we see its disk almost fully lighted by the sun, like the moon a day or so from full. But when Venus is near its minimum distance from us (left), its sunlit side is almost turned away from us. All we see is a slim crescent like the moon just before or after the date of new moon. (The moonlike phases can be seen through even a small telescope.)

The month-by-month calendar at the end of the book gives the magnitude of Venus at midmonth.

All the help you'll need in finding Venus is really to know only whether it is Morning Star or Evening Star. That's indicated by the following code:

A.M.   Venus visible before sunrise in the east
P.M.   Venus visible after sunset in the west
-o-   Venus too close to the sun for observation

The calendar also gives the approximate angle between the sun and Venus at midmonth in degrees.

When you see a line that reads:

Venus P.M.   40°   −3.8

you will know that Venus, now the Evening Star, is visible in the west all month long; on the fifteenth of the month it will be about four hands from the sun and of magnitude −3.8.

An entry that reads:

Venus P.M. to 7
A.M. after 22

will indicate to you that Venus is Evening Star until the seventh, then becomes unobservable until the twenty-second, when it emerges as Morning Star.

After the year 1990, when the calendar runs out, you are not without all help. Use the same month eight years earlier. *Example:* For March 1991 use March 1983.

Mercury is as hard to find as Venus is easy. Copernicus, who lived to be seventy, never managed to see it. You may want to skip Mercury and go on to Mars.

But some readers love a challenge. They deserve some guidance in observing Mercury.

Mercury's orbit, like that of Venus, is on the sunward side of Earth. But Mercury is much closer to the sun than Venus. Result: While Venus can get as far as 47° from the sun, Mercury can never get more than 28° away. Even that doesn't tell the whole story. Unlike the orbit of Venus, Mercury's orbit is quite elliptical. That makes that angle—*greatest elongation*—vary between 18° and 28°.

Unlike sedate Venus, Mercury zips around from evening to morning visibility six or seven times a year. That, in theory, gives you six or seven periods when you can see Mercury either in the east before sunrise or in the west after sunset—low in the sky in both cases.

And that is one of the problems with seeing Mercury. Atmospheric extinction near the horizon lowers its observed magnitude.

When the first stars come out in the evening, or the last stars fade in the morning, the sun is about 6 degrees below the horizon. Does that mean that Mercury, when its elongation is 18°, is 12 degrees above the horizon? It does not. The line from Mercury to the sun runs at an angle to the horizon and Mercury may be just kissing the horizon. Even at 28° elongation, Mercury may be barely above the horizon. The angle depends on the season and your latitude.

The result is that for a few days, or at most a few weeks, at some latitudes, Mercury is visible for at most one half hour in the morning or evening.

The calendar at the end of the book gives these periods. The criterion is the one used by the United States Naval Observatory: The elongation of Mercury must exceed 10°. Depending on your location, the period will be shorter; it may even be zero days.

The code used is similar to the one for Venus: A.M. for morning and easterly, P.M. for evening and westerly; -o- for too close to the sun for observation.

The angle of elongation is not given because it is rather meaningless for the individual observer. An 18° elongation may bring Mercury higher above the horizon than one of 28°.

In northern mid-latitudes the most favorable periods for observation of Mercury are: as an evening star shortly after the beginning of spring; as a morning star shortly after the beginning of autumn.

The magnitude given in the calendar refers to whatever date is mentioned on that line. *Example:* A.M. to 25 −0.5 means Mercury may be visible until the twenty-fifth, when its magnitude will be −0.5 (before correction for atmospheric extinction).

The following two rules may help you estimate how the magnitude of Mercury changes: As a morning star, Mercury brightens during its period of visibility; as an evening star, Mercury becomes dimmer toward the end of the period.

After the calendar expires, you can get rough indications of the periods of visibility of Mercury. Use the calendar for six years earlier, then add ten days to all dates given there.

Mars at times is hard to overlook, at other times hard to find. You already know the reason. Its magnitude changes from brighter than Jupiter's to that of Polaris.

At all times, as you already know, it is reddish. Only one first-magnitude star, Antares, near its apparent path is that red. At about two-year intervals the two rivals meet.

In the view of the planet orbits (Fig. 32) you can see that the orbit of Mars, unlike those of Mercury and Venus, lies outside the orbit of Earth. That lifts the restriction that keeps the inner planets, seen from Earth, to within so many degrees from the sun.

To the stargazer, that means that Mars will be visible not only before sunrise or after sunset, but at any time of the night. It also means: Not only will you see Mars at some easterly or westerly bearing, but it can bear south of you.

When Mars, seen from Earth, is close to the sun (at right in Fig. 35) you cannot see it. The motions of Earth and Mars combine for that to happen every other year and to last for several months. (You'll again find these periods indicated by the symbol -o- in the calendar.)

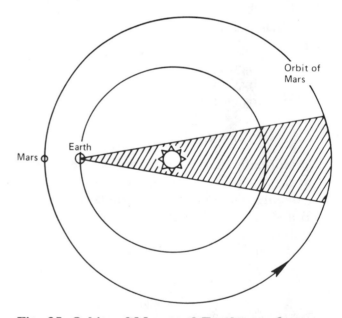

Fig. 35. Orbits of Mars and Earth seen from above.

When Mars emerges from the glare of the sun it is far from us, since the distance Earth–sun adds to the distance sun–Mars. That will make Mars appear dim.

Then the distance diminishes. Mars becomes brighter. The fact that at the same time less of the lighted side of Mars is turned toward us matters little. Unlike Venus and Mercury, Mars never appears half-lighted or crescent-shaped. At worst it looks like the moon a few days before or after full.

Mars will continue to brighten until it is nearest to Earth and fully lit. At that time Mars, seen from Earth, is opposite the sun. It will then bear south twelve hours after the sun, at midnight. The time from one such *opposition* to the next is two years and a few weeks.

As you can see in the illustration, the orbit of Mars is quite elliptical. So its distance from the sun and from us will differ from one opposition to the next, and with this, its magnitude. The most favorable opposition, shown in Figure 35, occurs every fifteen or seventeen years, when it falls in the month of August.

Here is a list of the next oppositions and the magnitude of Mars at these occasions:

1980	February 25	−0.9
1982	March 31	−1.1
1984	May 11	−1.7
1986	July 11	−2.4
1988	September 30	−2.5
1990	November 28	−1.8

Normally Mars in one month moves on the average about one hour in right ascension (roughly **one** and one-half hands) eastward. But strange things happen when Mars is near opposition.

If you could look down on the solar sys-tem, as in Figure 32, you'd see Earth (moving faster on the inner track) overtake Mars (moving more slowly on the outer track). Seen from Earth, Mars will first seem to stand still, then move backwards (to the west), and stand still again before taking up its normal eastward journey amid the stars.

The calendar at the end of the book gives the position of Mars (right ascension and declination) as well as its magnitude at about ten-day intervals. For example:

	RA	DEC	MAG
15	10.4	N12	+0.6

which decodes: On the fifteenth of this month, Mars is in right ascension 10.4^h and declination N12°. Its magnitude is +0.6.

You could pencil the position of Mars for the nearest date onto any star map (e.g., Figs. 11 or 12). Often such plotting will give a quick clue for finding the planet. In this case it will be right next to Regulus and noticeably brighter.

For your convenience, the position of the five first-magnitude stars near the ecliptic is printed at the bottom of every calendar page.

Jupiter is almost always the brightest star-like object after Venus. Only at a very favorable opposition does Mars get brighter than Jupiter at its brightest.

Like Mars, Jupiter can be at any angle to the sun. About every thirteen months Jupiter reaches opposition. It is then visible all night, bears south at midnight, and is of max-

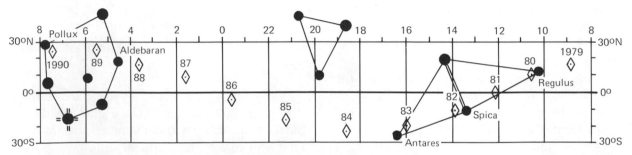

Fig. 36. Jupiter's midyear position among the stars.

imum brightness. Like Mars, it loops backwards at around that time.

For about one month each year, Jupiter gets too close to the sun for observation. Only just before and after these disappearances does Jupiter get dimmer than the brightest fixed star, Sirius.

Through a telescope, Jupiter always looks virtually full, so the change in magnitude is almost entirely due to its changing distance from Earth. At opposition it is only about four Earth–sun distances, called *astronomical units* (A.U.), from us. When it passes at the far side of the sun, at *conjunction,* the distance is about six astronomical units.

It takes Jupiter about twelve years to complete a tour around the sun. So in one year its right ascension increases by only about two hours. From one month to the next, Jupiter will usually have traveled only one finger east from where you saw it last. That makes keeping track of Jupiter comparatively easy.

The midyear position of Jupiter among the stars will give you a good clue to where to look for Jupiter.

The calendar lists Jupiter just like Mars, except that only the position for the middle of the month is given.

Here are the next oppositions of Jupiter and the magnitude of Jupiter at these dates:

1979	January 24	−2.2
1980	February 24	−2.1
1981	March 26	−2.0
1982	April 25	−2.0
1983	May 27	−2.1
1984	June 29	−2.2
1985	August 5	−2.3
1986	September 12	−2.4
1987	October 19	−2.5
1988	November 23	−2.4
1989	December 28	−2.3
1990	none	

Saturn is visible at some time of the night for about eleven months of the year, then becomes invisible for about one month. Most of the time it looks like a first-magnitude star of no particular color.

Yet it is easier to find than you'd expect. What helps in finding it is its very slow motion.

Of all the naked-eye planets, Saturn is the farthest from the sun, about ten times as far as the Earth. That gives it a long orbit to cover. And, according to the law of gravity, it moves more slowly in its orbit than nearer planets. Result: It takes Saturn about thirty years to circle the sun.

In one year it increases its right ascension

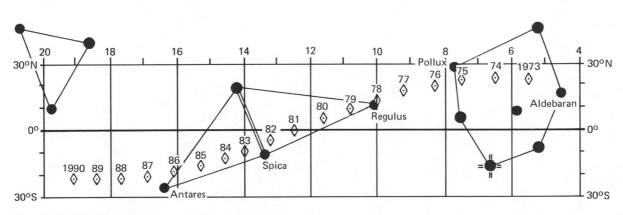

Fig. 37. Saturn's midyear position among the stars.

by less than one hour; that means it moves not much more than one hand eastward in one year. When you haven't watched the sky for some weeks or even months, you'll still find Saturn just about where you last saw it.

The sketch shows the midyear position of Saturn among the stars. The calendar gives position and magnitude of Saturn; the arrangement of data is the same as for Jupiter.

Only a small part of Saturn's wide range of magnitude is explained by the planet's changing distance from us. Like Mars and Jupiter, it is at its brightest at opposition, when it bears south at midnight. It is dimmest just before and after its disappearance behind the sun, when it rises or sets in twilight.

Saturn's distance from us, which has been $8\frac{1}{2}$ A.U. at opposition, will then be $10\frac{1}{2}$ times our distance from the sun. That accounts only for a change of a few tenths of one magnitude.

The greater part of the change—Saturn always appears virtually full—is due to its spectacular rings. When they appear wide open they are brighter than the planet itself. When they are edge on to the sun or when they are edge on to Earth, they contribute nothing to the apparent magnitude of Saturn. At all other times the rings add varying amounts of light to the overall brightness of Saturn, depending on their width seen from Earth.

A complete cycle from ringless to wide-open rings to again ringless takes $29\frac{1}{2}$ years. In 1980 Saturn will be ringless; in 1987 the rings will appear at their widest, Saturn at its brightest.

You can trace the contribution of the rings in the following table of oppositions. The opposition magnitude around 1987 (though nowhere near the maximum magnitude of Saturn) is obviously brighter than that of 1980.

Here are the next oppositions of Saturn and its magnitude at these dates:

1979	March 1	+0.5
1980	March 13	+0.8
1981	March 27	+0.7
1982	April 8	+0.5
1983	April 21	+0.4
1984	May 3	+0.3
1985	May 16	+0.2
1986	May 28	+0.2
1987	June 10	+0.2
1988	June 20	+0.2
1989	July 2	+0.2
1990	July 14	+0.2

7

The Moon; More Stars and Constellations

You may want to learn more stars and constellations. For that you'll need moon-dark hours of the night. That's the reason for having a quick look at the moon.

The Moon

On the scale of magnitude we have used for stars and planets the full moon rates − 12. On a night when it is full the moon blots out all but the brightest stars and the planets. On that night it is up during all hours the sun is down: a very bad night for finding constellation patterns and dimmer stars.

Everyone knows that the moon goes through phases. You can demonstrate how they come about by using a tennis ball for the moon and the sun itself or a flashlight for the sun.

When you stand between the light source and the ball (without casting your shadow on it), you see the ball fully lighted, like a full moon.

When you are on the opposite side—you, the ball, and the light source in line—you only see the unlighted part of the ball, as at new moon.

When you stand at right angles to the light-to-ball line, to the left or to the right, you see one half of the ball lighted, the other half dark. The ball appears like the moon at first or last quarter.

Don't let the word *quarter* bother you. It means the phase when the moon is *half* lighted. (Calendars and newspapers add to the confusion by traditionally showing the half moon as a crescent.) We call them quarters because these phases come at one quarter and three quarters in the complete cycle, which lasts about one month ($29\frac{1}{4}$ to $29\frac{3}{4}$ days).

First quarter, then, is about a week after the *new* moon; last quarter about one week after *full* moon.

Which side of the moon is missing at which quarter? Schoolboys in ancient Rome had a simple memory aid: *The moon is a liar*. When it looks like a letter *D*, it is *not* decreasing. When it looks like a *C*, it is. I can't find an English word that means increasing and starts with a *C*. Will you settle for this? When it resembles a letter *G*, it is *not* growing, but diminishing.

For stargazing you don't care much about the phases of the moon as such, but want to know when the moon will be above your horizon at night. The two phenomena are closely linked.

Let's look at the connection, neglecting fractions of days and making the phases seven days apart. It's easier to remember that way.

Traditionally one starts with *new moon*—age of moon zero days. You won't see the moon (except during an eclipse of the sun, when it gets between you and the sun). In most months the moon just misses eclipsing the sun; but it's swallowed up by the glare of the sun. The moon on that day will rise with the sun, be south with the sun—at noon—and set with the sun.

You probably won't become aware of the moon until a couple of days later. It then forms a thin crescent, east of the sun, and unlighted on the eastern side. (It's working up to look like a letter *D*.)

Being a little east of the sun, it will set not long after the sun, not spoiling the viewing of stars. The exact time of moonset (and moonrise, too) depends—like those of sunset and sunrise—on your latitude and on how far north or south of the celestial equator the moon (or sun) happens to be on a given day.

The moon seen from the same place on Earth rises later each day. The delay varies from a few minutes to more than one hour. The moon will then stay up somewhat longer in your western sky while it gets fatter: more elegantly, while it is in the *waxing crescent* phase.

By the time it is about a week old—at *first quarter*—with its eastern half still dark, it

Phase: New moon
Age: 0 days South: Noon
Dark: All night

Phase: Waxing crescent
Dark: All but first hours

Phase: First quarter
Age: 7 days South: 6 P.M.
Dark: Last half of night

Phase: Waxing gibbous
Dark: Last hours of night

Phase: Full moon
Age: 14 days South: Midnight
Dark: No time of night

Phase: Waning gibbous
Dark: First hours of night

Phase: Last quarter
Age: 21 days South: 6 A.M.
Dark: First half of night

Phase: Waning crescent
Dark: All but last hours

Phase: New moon
Age: 29 days = 0 days
see top of figure

Fig. 38. Phases of the moon.

will be due south of you at about 6 P.M. and will be quite bright during the evening hours.

Then, rising and setting later each day, it gets more rounded. A moon that's more than half lighted is called *gibbous* (sounded like "give us"). During the *waxing gibbous* phase the moon will interfere with your star watching during all but the last hours of the night.

About two weeks after new moon, one week after first quarter, the moon will be fully lighted, opposite the sun. The *full moon,* having risen at sunset, and due to set at sunrise, will bear south at midnight. That spoils watching stars all night long.

After having been full, the moon begins to look eaten away on the western side, *waning gibbous.* It rises after sunset. In a few days you'll have some time of darkness before moonrise.

About a week after full moon, three weeks after new moon, the moon will be half lighted, dark on the western side—looking like a *C* or *G,* if you like—*last quarter.* You'll have the first half of the night for moonless stargazing.

The moon will continue to rise later—and give you more hours for star watching—as it goes through the *waning crescent* phase.

About four weeks after the last new moon, two weeks after full, the moon will again disappear in the glare of the sun: another new moon. Then the cycle starts all over.

To help you plan your stargazing, the calendar at the end of the book gives the dates of new moon, first quarter, full moon, and last quarter in the order in which they fall in any given month. When, say, a new moon occurs at the very beginning of a month, there may be a second new moon at the end of the month. To suit the needs of the majority of my readers I have adjusted the dates—supplied by the Science Research Council—to the Eastern Standard Time zone.

(*Explanation:* When full moon occurs on February 12 at 2:40 A.M., Greenwich Time, it is still February 11 in New York and Montreal, and also in San Francisco and Vancouver.)

Constellations of the Zodiac

In the dark of the moon, having mastered the planets and the brighter constellations, you may want to look for more constellations.

What, for instance, about the constellations of the zodiac? Their names are familiar to millions who couldn't tell Venus from Vega.

Zodiac literally means the "circle of animals" (you recognize the root *zoo*). There are some strange animals in this zoological collection:

LATIN NAME	PRONUNCIATION	ENGLISH NAME
Aries	AR-eez or AR-ee-ez	Ram
Taurus	TO-ruhs	Bull
Gemini	JEM-i-neye or -nee	Twins
Cancer	KAN-suhr	Crab
Leo	LEE-oh	Lion
Virgo	VUHR-goh	Virgin
Libra	LEYE-bruh or LEE-bruh	Scales
Scorpius	SKOR-pi-uhs	Scorpion
Sagittarius	saj-i-TAY-ri-uhs	Archer
Capricornus	kap-ri-KOR-nuhs	Sea Goat
Aquarius	uh-KWAY-ri-uhs	Water Carrier
Pisces	PIS-eez or PEYE-suhs	Fishes

When the Babylonians some four thousand years ago started all this, the sun at the beginning of the year, the beginning of spring, crossed the celestial equator in Aries. From that point they divided the annual path of the sun into twelve equal parts and named the "signs" after the constellation through which the sun passed during each month-long period.

That didn't work well even for the Babylonians. The constellation Virgo, for example, stretches three times as far as the constellation Cancer.

Today it doesn't work at all. Since Hipparchus, who lived in the second century B.C., the Western world has known that the sun at the beginning of spring crosses the celestial equator a little farther west than the

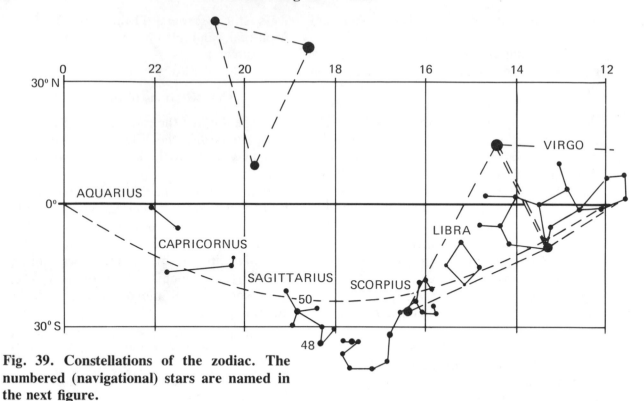

Fig. 39. Constellations of the zodiac. The numbered (navigational) stars are named in the next figure.

year before. (In about 26,000 years it comes back to the same point.) You can call that the *precession of the vernal equinox* if you like learned terms.

More than two thousand years ago the crossing point—still called the First Point of Aries, or Aries for short—moved completely out of the constellation Aries, and into Pisces. It soon will slip out of Pisces and into Aquarius.

If your birthday is April 1, the sun was in the constellation Pisces when you were born. But by your "sign" you are still an Aries. When the sun comes to be in Aquarius on that date, people born that day will still be called Aries.

You can find five of the constellations of the zodiac from their first-magnitude stars. Those are the five stars—all of magnitude 1.2—we used as a help in finding the planets in the last chapter.

The other constellations of the zodiac are far from prominent. Only two of the remaining seven have even second-magnitude stars in them. Sagittarius—next to the tail of Scorpius—sports two, Kaus Australis (KOS os-TRAY-lis), no. 48, and Nunki (NUHN-kee), no. 50. (You'll read about these numbers in a moment.)

Aries has one second-magnitude star, Hamal (HAM-uhl), no. 6. You'll find it by measuring about three hands from the Square of Pegasus toward Aldebaran.

Dimmer Stars

You may have thought me arbitrary for emphasizing first-magnitude stars and seemingly slighting second-magnitude stars and fainter ones.

But I have not slighted them as much as it seemed. Here and there I have slipped in quite a few second-magnitude and fainter stars. Very early I introduced Castor—only a

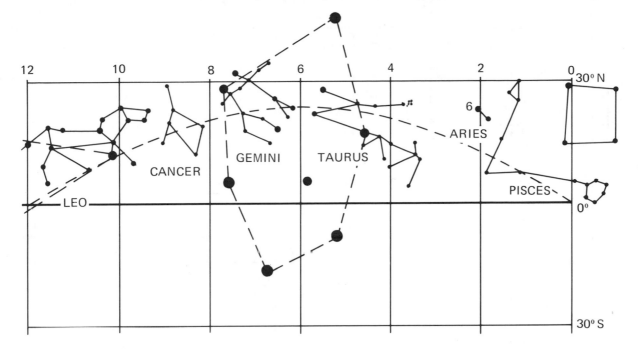

little dimmer than its twin, Pollux—the constellation Orion, and the Square of Pegasus. That's quite a few stars of less than first magnitude.

In the constellations you can find from their bright stars, you met many more dimmer stars. And all the stars in the polar cap were of second (or third) magnitude.

Constellation	First-mag. Star	Other clues
Aries	—	Hamal (6)
Taurus	Aldebaran	
Gemini	Pollux	
Cancer	—	Between Gemini and Leo
Leo	Regulus	
Virgo	Spica	
Libra	—	Between Virgo and Scorpius
Scorpius	Antares	
Sagittarius	—	Kaus Australis (48) and Nunki (50)
Capricornus	—	East of Sagittarius
Aquarius	—	Between Square of Pegasus and Fomalhaut
Pisces	—	On celestial equator, west of Aries

Fig. 40. Finding the constellations of the zodiac. The numbered (navigational) stars are shown in Fig. 39.

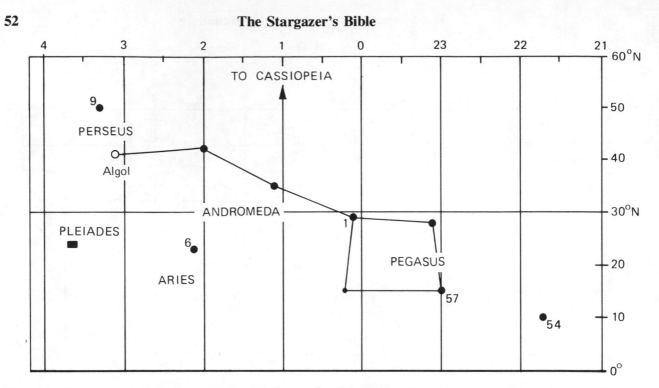

Fig. 41. Dimmer stars in the vicinity of the Square of Pegasus. The area is shown enlarged from the scale used in other star maps in this book. Numbers refer to navigational stars, listed in Fig. 44.

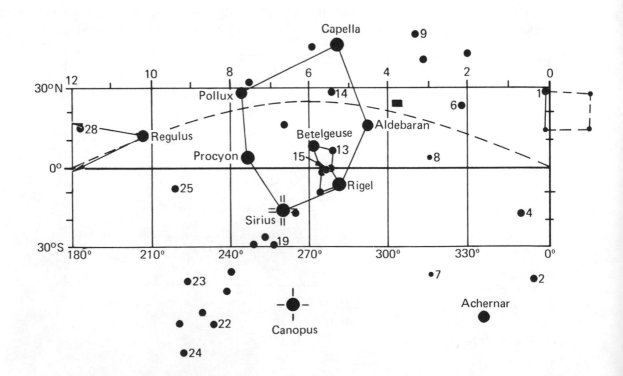

All told, you have already met more than half of all second-magnitude stars.

Here are a few more. You may see another dipper shape in the vicinity of the Square of Pegasus. The star near the zero hour line, labeled 1, called Alpheratz (al-FEE-rats), is shared between the constellations Pegasus and Andromeda (an-DROM-uh-duh). The next two stars in the handle belong to Andromeda; the star at the end of the handle, Algol (AL-gol) , is in Perseus (PUHR-see-uhs).

All the second-magnitude stars within the strip chart are shown in Figure 42. (All such stars even farther north appear in the polar cap, Figure 28.)

All the southern second-magnitude stars you are likely to notice in the Northern Hemisphere—and well into the Tropics—are also shown. Most of the time these stars, even where they are above the horizon, will be too low in the sky to look like second-

magnitude objects. The best time to watch for them is when they are highest in the sky: that is, when they are about due south of you.

Quite a few of these stars are in what used to be the constellation Argo (AR-goh), the Ship. That means they are in the modern constellations Puppis (PUHP-is), the Stern, or Vela (VEE-luh), the Sails, or Carina (kuh-REYE-nuh), the Keel. (Canopus, the second-brightest fixed star, is also in Carina.) These stars will be south of you after the ones in Canis Major, including Sirius. Look for them when local star time is between 8^h and 9$\frac{1}{2}^h$.

Navigational Stars

Your interest in stars may be for use in celestial navigation. That's the method by which—on land, in the air, but mostly at

Fig. 42. Star map of second-magnitude and navigational stars visible in the coverage area. Northernmost stars appear in Fig. 28.

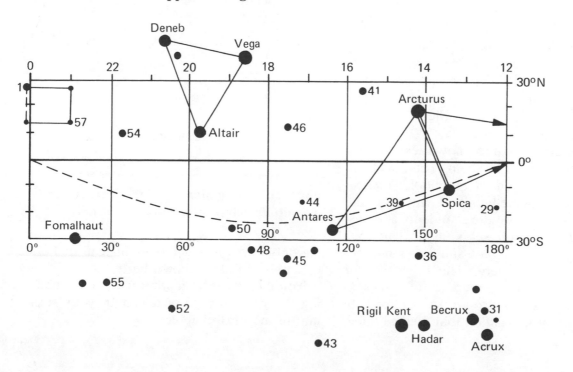

sea—you get your location by measuring with a sextant the height of stars above your horizon.

Do you already know enough stars for that? The answer is pleasant: You already know more stars than you'll ever need.

Most navigators "shoot" three stars in rapid succession. Every navigator will shoot stars that are listed in the daily pages of the Nautical Almanac (or Air Almanac). All but one of the first-magnitude stars are listed there. (Becrux is the exception; but its neighbors Acrux and Gacrux (GAY-kruhks) are listed.)

Navigators avoid taking sights of stars close to the horizon or almost overhead. Even with these restrictions you could probably navigate all your life and all over the world with just first-magnitude stars and a few easily found second-magnitude stars— say, in Cassiopeia or the Big Dipper— especially since you can also use the planets Venus, Mars, Jupiter, and Saturn for "star" sights.

Many navigators use the star volume (Volume I) of the *Sight Reduction Tables for Air Navigation* (H.O. Publication No. 249, published by the U. S. Naval Oceanographic Office, or the identical British publication AP 3270). These tables, very useful for yachtsmen, list seven suitably placed stars for any given time of observation. To get you *seven* stars at any one time, wherever you may be from pole to pole, the tables use a total of forty-one stars.

But you don't have to know these stars by name to be able to find them. You can cheat, as I have described in my book *Practical Navigation* (Doubleday & Company) and taught to several hundred students of celestial navigation. You set your sextant to a figure given in the tables and face the direction also printed there. The brightest star you'll then see in the eyepiece of your sextant is almost certain to be the right one. In many years of navigation that method failed

MAG	Star	#
3.1	Acamar	7
1.6	Adhara	19
1.7	Alioth	32
1.9	Alkaid	34
2.2	Al Na'ir	55
1.8	Alnilam	15
2.2	Alphard	25
2.3	Alphecca	41
2.2	Alpheratz	1
2.4	Ankaa	2
1.9	Atria	43
1.7	Avior	22
1.7	Bellatrix	13
2.2	Denebola	28
2.2	Diphda	4
2.0	Dubhe	27
1.8	Elnath	14
2.4	Eltanin	47
2.5	Enif	54
1.6	Gacrux	31
2.8	Gienah	29
2.2	Hamal	6
2.0	Kaus Australis	48
2.2	Kochab	40
2.6	Markab	57
2.8	Menkar	8
2.3	Menkent	36
1.8	Miaplacidus	24
1.9	Mirfak	9
2.1	Nunki	50
2.1	Peacock	52
2.1	Rasalhague	46
2.6	Sabik	44
2.5	Schedar	3
1.7	Shaula	45
2.2	Suhail	23
2.9	Zubenelgenubi	39

Fig. 43. Navigational stars (except first-magnitude stars) in alphabetical order.

me only once: I shot Castor instead of Pollux. I should have known better.

You'll read about another method for finding the right navigational star in your sextant in the next chapter.

#	Star	MAG	Pronunciation	Constellation
1	Alpheratz	2.2	al-FEE-rats	Andromeda
2	Ankaa	2.4	AN-kuh	Phoenix
3	Schedar	2.5	SHED-uhr	Cassiopeia
4	Diphda	2.2	DIF-duh	Cetus
6	Hamal	2.2	HAM-uhl	Aries
7	Acamar	3.1	AY-kuh-mar	Eridanus
8	Menkar	2.8	MEN-kar	Cetus
9	Mirfak	1.9	MEER-fak	Perseus
13	Bellatrix	1.7	bel-LAY-tricks	Orion
14	Elnath	1.8	EL-nath	Taurus
15	Alnilam	1.8	AL-ni-lam	Orion
19	Adhara	1.6	a-DAY-ra	Canis Major
22	Avior	1.7	AY-vi-or	Carina
23	Suhall	2.2	soo-HAYL	Vela
24	Miaplacidus	1.0	MEYE a PLAS i duha	Carina
25	Alphard	2.2	AL-fard	Hydra
27	Dubhe	2.0	DUHB-ee or DOO-bee	Ursa Major
28	Denebola	2.2	de-NEB-oh-luh	Leo
29	Gienah	2.8	JEE-na	Corvus
31	Gacrux	1.6	GAY-kruhks	Crux
32	Alioth	1.7	AL-i-oth	Ursa Major
34	Alkaid	1.9	al-KAYD	Ursa Major
36	Menkent	2.3	MEN-kent	Centaurus
39	Zubenelgenubi	2.9	zoo-BEN-el-je-NOO-bee	Libra
40	Kochab	2.2	KOH-kab	Ursa Minor
41	Alphecca	2.3	al-FEK-uh	Corona Borealis
43	Atria	1.9	AT-ri-uh	Triangulum Australe
44	Sabik	2.6	SAY-bik	Ophiuchus
45	Shaula	1.7	SHO-luh	Scorpius
46	Rasalhague	2.1	RAS-al-HAYG-wee	Ophiuchus
47	Eltanin	2.4	el-TAY-nin	Draco
48	Kaus Australis	2.0	KOS os-TRAY-lis	Sagittarius
50	Nunki	2.1	NUHN-kee	Sagittarius
52	Peacock	2.1	PEE-kok	Pavo
54	Enif	2.5	EN-if	Pegasus
55	Al Na'ir	2.2	al-NAYR	Grus
57	Markab	2.6	MAR-kab	Pegasus

Fig. 44. Navigational stars in numerical order. (Numbers of first-magnitude navigational stars are given in Fig. 73.)

The only time a navigator needs to know more stars than you already know would be during an examination that requires knowledge of all fifty-seven navigational stars. Six of them are third-magnitude stars. Polaris is not included in the fifty-seven navigational stars because it is usually worked by a different method of sight reduction.

All the navigational stars are shown in Figures 42 and 28. First-magnitude stars are identified by name, all others by their official number. Should you ever need to know the numbers of first-magnitude stars, you'll find them in Figure 73.

The numbers increase with increasing right ascension from no. 1 for Alpheratz (RA 0.1^h) to no. 57 for Markab (23.0^h). That helps when you want to locate a numbered star on any of the star maps in this book, or elsewhere.

But modern navigators and the Nautical Almanac don't use right ascension any more. Instead they use a closely related measure: the star's hour angle, or *sidereal hour angle*, abbreviated SHA. It is measured in degrees rather than in hours. The conversion is easy: 1 hour = 15°. Both systems start from the same zero point. The First Point of Aries (the vernal equinox) is 0.0^h RA and 000° SHA. But the two scales run in opposite directions. That makes 2^h RA 330° SHA; 4^h RA 300° SHA. To save you the calculation, in Figure 42 the hour lines labeled in the usual way in RA on top are labeled in SHA at the bottom.

If your interest is in *constellations* rather than individual stars, the numbered stars will lead you to another dozen constellations.

8

Star Maps and Star Finders

You may have wondered: Why bother with finding the celestial equator, getting local star time, and all that? Isn't there an easier way to find or identify stars and constellations? Isn't there some visual aid that lets me match the sky I see with the stars and outlines of constellations?

There have been many ingenious attempts to solve that problem, none perfect. Let's look at some of them.

You can almost from the beginning eliminate star globes. They show the star sphere from the *outside,* just as the familiar globes show the earth from the outside. But you are looking at the star sphere from the *inside*. That makes matching globe to sky, or the other way around, quite awkward. Also, such a globe is cumbersome when you walk your dog or paddle a canoe. And it is fairly expensive.

What you really want, I believe, is a *flat,* easily portable, inexpensive stargazer's aid.

Monthly Star Maps

Natural History magazine prints a circular star map for the current month in every issue. It shows the night sky as it appears when you are lying on your back, looking straight up. That's great for the stars near your zenith. But in that position you'd miss seeing all the stars that are in the sky between your horizon and, say, three hands from the zenith.

To see these stars and compare them with the map, do this: Hold the star map so that the direction you are facing is at the bottom. The stars nearest the bottom of the map will then match the ones near your horizon. Say you start by facing north; hold the map so that *N* is on the bottom.

Then turn, say, south and bring *S* to the bottom. You may want to check groups of stars in the northwest, Cygnus and Cas-

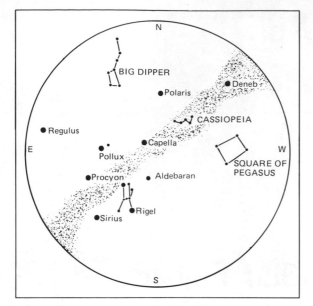

Fig. 45. Star map as in *Natural History* **magazine.**

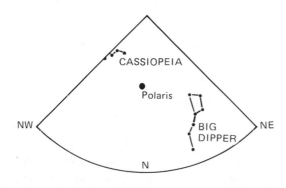

Fig. 46. Holding circular star map when facing north.

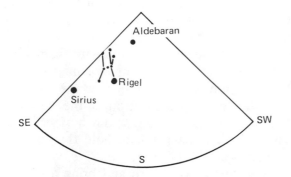

Fig. 47. Holding circular star map when facing south.

siopeia; just bring the space between *N* and *W* to the bottom.

The Milky Way is suggested on this map; the major constellations are shown geometrically.

In a December issue, say, of *Natural History* you will find a map that matches the sky at 10:20 P.M. (local time) on December 15, at 9:20 P.M. on December 31, and at 8:20 P.M. on January 15. A note tells you that the map can also be used for one hour before and after these times. All times are, strictly speaking, *local* times, but at most locations standard time will be accurate enough.

By January 15 you should have received the January issue with the star map drawn for, say, 10:20 on January 15. . . .

If you have subscribed to this magazine for at least a year (or can borrow a year's issues) you are not tied to these hours of observation. You know that at any one location whether and where in the sky a star is visible depends on your star time. Find the star time for the nearest civil time of observation in Figure 48.

Example: December 31 at about 9:30 gives star time 4^h. The map mentioned above for December 31 at 9:20 P.M. is obviously also drawn for 4^h star time. You can use it for any combination of date and time where you find a figure 4. For example, around September 1, at 5:30 A.M., or November 15, at 12:30 A.M.

With a year's copies of star maps you'll have a map for every two hours of every night, each map usable for one hour earlier or later. So you are all set for every hour of every night. In this recycling you'll have to ignore the position of the planets and the moon and its phases. They do *not* repeat year after year.

These sky maps, although it is not specifically stated, are drawn for the sky as it appears in latitude 40°N. If you live in that latitude or near it—say, between 35°N and 45°N—they are fine for you.

DATE	EVENING HOURS						MORNING HOURS						
	6:30	7:30	8:30	9:30	10:30	11:30	12:30	1:30	2:30	3:30	4:30	5:30	6:30
Jan. 1		2		4		6		8		10		12	
15	2		4		6		8		10		12		14
Feb. 1		4		6		8		10		12		14	
15	4		6		8		10		12		14		16
Mar. 1		6		8		10		12		14		16	
15	6		8		10		12		14		16		18
Apr. 1		8		10		12		14		16		18	
15	8		10		12		14		16		18		20
May 1		10		12		14		16		18		20	
15	10		12		14		16		18		20		22
June 1		12		14		16		18		20		22	
15	12		14		16		18		20		22		0
July 1		14		16		18		20		22		0	
15	14		16		18		20		22		0		2
Aug. 1		16		18		20		22		0		2	
15	16		18		20		22		0		2		4
Sep. 1		18		20		22		0		2		4	
15	18		20		22		0		2		4		6
Oct. 1		20		22		0		2		4		6	
15	20		22		0		2		4		6		8
Nov. 1		22		0		2		4		6		8	
15	22		0		2		4		6		8		10
Dec. 1		0		2		4		6		8		10	
15	0		2		4		6		8		10		12
31		2		4		6		8		10		12	

Fig. 48. Table of even hours of star time that lets you use star maps at other than indicated times.

Sky and Telescope magazine also publishes a monthly star map. Rather than a single circle, the map looks like four overlapping circles. All the circles share the east and west points. The four circles indicate the observer's horizon in latitudes 50, 40, 30, and 20°N. In or near latitude 40°N you'd use the north horizon marked 40° and the south horizon with the same marking.

If you live permanently in, say, latitude 30° you may save confusion by emphasizing with a felt-tip pen the 30° horizon, north and south. The use of the circle chosen is identical to the one described before: Hold the magazine so the direction you are facing is at the bottom.

The zenith for each circle is not marked on the star map. But it's easily found. On the North–South line of the map, which is graduated (for declination) at 10-degree intervals,

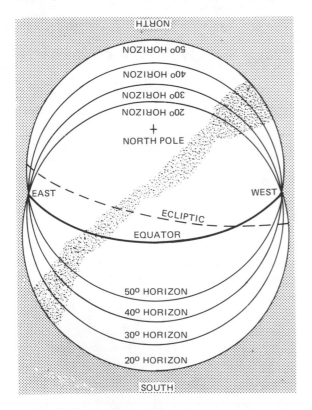

Fig. 49. Diagram of star map as in *Sky and Telescope*.

find the number that corresponds to your latitude. (A plus sign here means north.) In latitude 30°N you'd look for the +30° mark. It will be near, but not at, the center of your horizon "circle," which is really an oval. You could emphasize that zenith point with a pen to mark your permanent location's zenith.

The map in the January issue of *Sky and Telescope* is for the evening hours as follows:

Early January	9 o'clock
Late January	8 o'clock
Early February	7 o'clock

From the table you can see that this map, too, is drawn for 4^h star time. If you have a year's collection of issues of this magazine, you have a star chart for every other hour of every night by recycling the maps according to the table in Figure 48.

You don't have to disregard planets and moon on these maps. They are shown on a separate map each month.

You'll find a similar collection of circular star maps for the entire year and three different latitudes (30, 40, and 50°N) in H. A. Rey's book *The Stars: A New Way to See Them* (Houghton Mifflin Company). They, too, are drawn for even hours of local star time. A key tells you which star map to use at what local time for every two weeks. Strictly speaking, the times are again local time. But you probably won't be far wrong using standard time. (But do subtract one hour from your time when you are on daylight saving time, for this and all other conversions.)

Actually, you'll find two star maps for every other hour of star time. The left page shows stars and the Milky Way. The right page shows constellations, drawn, of course, in Mr. Rey's imaginative manner. That page also shows the ecliptic, near which you'll find the planets Mars, Jupiter, and Saturn if they are visible at all.

You may want to pencil in the zenith at the

approximate center of the circle that corresponds to the latitude of your permanent residence.

By now you may wonder whether a book, or a set of twelve maps from a magazine, and the finding of star time from approximate date and time are the answer for you. Isn't there a simpler way?

There is.

Star Finders

A star finder, or planisphere, is a simple mechanical device that shows for a given latitude the stars that are above the horizon at any given local civil time and date.

It consists of a circular star map that rotates under a fixed mask, which represents your horizon. The two parts are usually held together by a rivet at the celestial pole. You *set* the star finder by bringing together the date (on the map) and the time (on the fixed part).

There are many such star finders available. They vary in size and detail; one even has stars that glow in the dark. The cost, at this time, ranges from $1.00 (Edmund Scientific Co.) upward.

The star map part shows stars down to a certain magnitude that are sometimes visible in the latitude for which the star finder has been designed. That map is centered on the celestial pole, unlike the circular star maps we have looked at before, which are centered on your zenith. That brings Polaris under the rivet.

The cutout, or mask, is an oval calculated for the designed latitude. The zenith for that latitude is near the center of the oval. Just remembering that is probably all you need to identify a constellation near the zenith at your location.

You could also make two marks on the mask, level with a point halfway between north and south. These marks will be near the widest part of the cutout, and below the

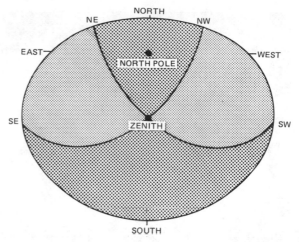

Fig. 50. Star finder: location of compass points on the horizon oval. Compare the shapes of the sectors between SE and SW with Fig. 47; between NW and NE, with Fig. 46.

points labeled east and west. The zenith at the latitude for which the star finder was designed will then be where a line between your marks crosses a line from south to the rivet. You can refine the position for *your* latitude after identifying a star at your zenith; just raise or lower the marks to make them level with that star.

Basically, you still hold the star finder with the direction you are facing at the bottom. But look closer: East is not where you might expect, on the long axis of the oval. Instead, it is at the height of Polaris. And so is west. The neat equal pieces of the pie now have strange shapes.

That distortion, shown by the odd pieces of pie, the lack of a zenith unless you provide it, and the restriction to a single latitude may make the usual standard star finder less than perfect for your latitude.

The latitude restriction has been partly overcome in a recently produced model, called *The Night Sky,* distributed by Sky Publishing Corporation, the publishers of *Sky and Telescope.* It is a series of *three* star finders (currently $2.00 apiece) as follows:

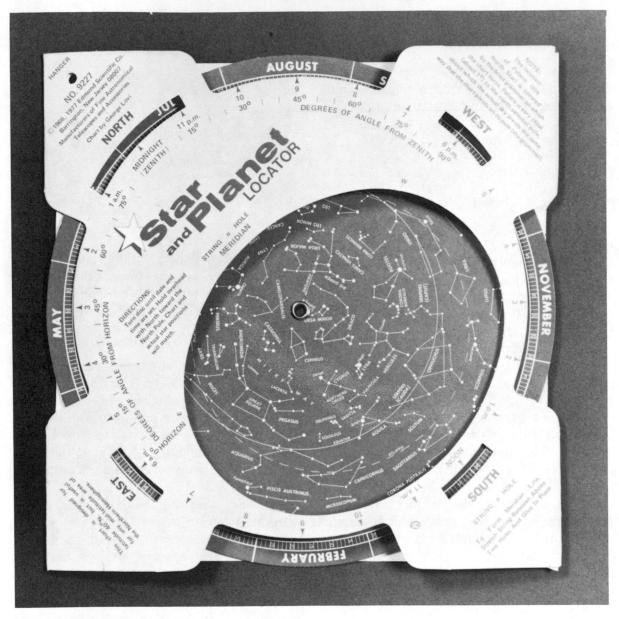

**Photo 1. Edmund star finder. Photo: Edmund
Scientific Co.**

Latitude Range	Designed for Lat.	Coverage Area in North America
20–32°N	25°N	Hawaii, Florida, southern Texas
30–40°N	35°N	Southern half of United States
38–50°N	40°N	Upper States and southern Canada

These star finders have *two* cutouts—one in front and one in back—and two star maps printed on opposite sides of the usual rotating disk. The Milky Way and the magnitude of stars are nicely marked; some objects best seen through binoculars are also shown. So are the celestial equator, the ecliptic, and even star time.

For use, you set the date to the time when you are watching the sky. Turn the side with

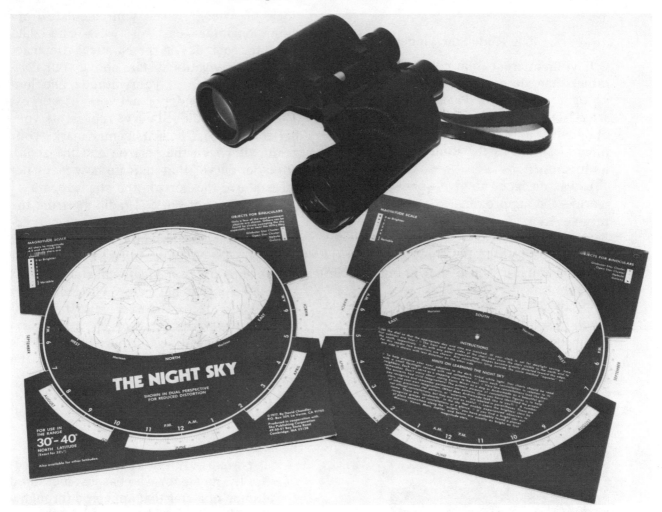

Photo 2. "The Night Sky" star finder. Photo: David & Janet Chandler.

the south horizon up and you'll see the stars from east through south to west displayed. Then turn the star finder over and face north. You'll see the stars from west through north to east.

Unfortunately, this side of the star finder also shows the southern sky, which of course you can't see when you face north. Perhaps that will be corrected in a future edition of this useful star finder.

Meanwhile, it would be helpful to mark the zenith, beyond which you obviously can't see. To do that, turn the disk until one

of the four scales numbered for declination is straight up and down above the north horizon. Locate your latitude on that scale. (*Example:* in latitude 30°N, find declination 30°; ignore declinations marked minus.) Make a mark left or right, or both, on the cutout level with that latitude. Regardless of the setting, your zenith will always be at that height, straight above Polaris (at the rivet).

On the south part of the star finder, the mask cuts off the sky at the zenith (for the latitude for which the star finder has been designed).

The Rude Star Finder

If your interest is in celestial navigation, rather than stargazing, you may want to investigate the *Star-Finder and Identifier* #2102-D (U. S. Navy Hydrographic Office), obtainable at nautical supply stores. Old-timers know it as the Rude star finder after its inventor.

It was designed to give—anywhere in the world—the approximate position of the fifty-seven navigational stars, which you met in the preceding chapter.

And those are all the stars it shows. The celestial equator is also shown, but no ecliptic and no Milky Way.

To allow for your approximate latitude—north or south of the equator—you place one of nine transparent overlays over a pin in the center of the plastic star map. You set it, not by time and date, but by the "local hour

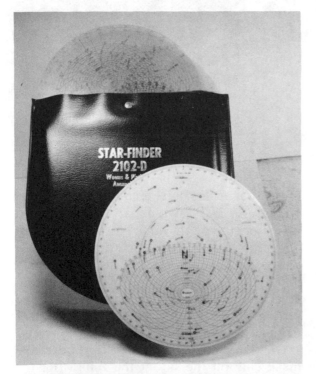

Photo 3. Rude star finder. Photo: Weems & Plath, Inc.

angle of Aries,'' which you calculate from your longitude—east or west—and data given for each day in the Nautical Almanac.

All the navigational stars above your horizon at that time at your latitude and longitude appear under a network of curves. The outermost closed curve represents your horizon. A cross near its center marks your zenith. Between the horizon and the zenith are other curves that indicate how many degrees above the horizon the star appears.

Another set of curves, radiating from the zenith, gives the azimuth (bearing or direction) of the star at that time, at your location.

This device could be called a calculator for the position of the navigational stars. This is how it helps the navigator: Guided by his compass, he faces the exact direction indicated by the star finder; he then sets his sextant to the angle above the horizon, the star's altitude. The brightest star he sees in the telescope of his sextant is likely to be the desired star. (A planet could still fool him, and he still might get Castor instead of Pollux.) That explains the *finder* part in the name of the device.

It is perhaps even more useful as an *identifier* for the navigator who has just measured the altitude of a star that appeared through a break in the clouds. There were not enough other stars visible to identify constellations or asterisms. He notes in what direction the star was observed, perhaps with a hand bearing-compass.

Finding the crossing point of the proper altitude and bearing curves on the star finder, set for his location and time, he finds the name of the star just observed.

For the general stargazer this clever device is of limited use. It calculates the position of a relatively small number of stars. It ignores constellations and does not permit you any visual comparison between map and sky: A star to the *left* of another in the sky is shown to the *right* on the Rude star finder. The cost of the many overlays and the vinyl carrying case drives the price up (currently $12.00).

But you may have inherited one of these devices or be able to borrow one from a sea-going friend. The instructions are probably missing; in any case, they are written in incomprehensible navigationalese.

Proceed as follows. Select the overlay closest to your latitude. In latitude 37°N, you'd use the 35° overlay. If the notation "Latitude 35°S" is now legible, turn the overlay over to make "Latitude 35°N" read properly, not in mirror writing. Place the overlay on the pin in the center of the star map that has a big *N* there (because you are in a northern latitude).

To get the proper setting, get your local star time from Figure 48. Then multiply the result (in hours) by 15 (to get degrees).

Set the arrow, which indicates south, to that figure on the outer rim of the star map.

Example: You find approximate local star time to be 4^h; 4 × 15 = 60; set the arrow to 60°. You'll find Rigel, for instance, bearing 150° (between SE and S) and a little more than 50° (five hands) above your horizon.

Another Visual Aid

Quite a different approach to helping you find or identify stars is taken by Donald H. Menzel in *A Field Guide to the Stars and Planets* (Houghton Mifflin Company).

You get two views of the sky that look almost like photographs (Milky Way included), one looking north, one south.

This book uses many dot sizes to indicate the magnitude of stars (ten besides the ones for Sirius and Canopus) down to magnitude 4.5. That gives the stars a most realistic appearance.

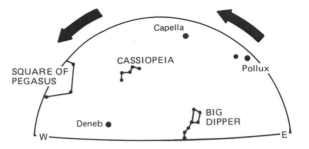

Fig. 51. A northern night sky view like those in *A Field Guide to the Stars and Planets*.

Facing the north or south view is an identical view with outlines of constellations (Rey's), names, equator, and ecliptic added.

The problem of different latitudes (15°–55°N) is neatly solved by a system of masks, one set for every 5 degrees of latitude. You'll need two masks, one for facing north, one for south. A sheet of tracing paper and a few minutes' work with pencil and scissors will make the masks for your latitude. (For latitude 35°N, you use the same mask for both the north and the south views.)

The *Field Guide* has twelve sets of sky views for the northern hemisphere, each set consisting of north and south views, plain and with labels. So you have an exact view for every two hours of star time (0, 2, 4^h . . .). A table gives the map numbers to use. But you can do better than that. As explained in that book, you can shift your masks to give the view at any precise local star time. You can adjust it easily to the nearest quarter hour, by calculation or directly from the stars themselves.

You may like these views better than star finders.

9

Stargazing in Other Areas

Now that you have been introduced to several visual aids for finding or identifying stars and constellations, let's look back at the system used in all the earlier chapters.

We have covered a large part of the sky by the basic strip map centered on the celestial equator. It's in that area that all the planets (and the moon) appear, and where you'll find fifteen of the twenty-one first-magnitude stars.

We have covered much of the rest of the sky, the northern part, with the polar cap.

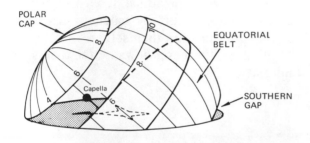

Fig. 52. Coverage of the dome of the sky by two star maps in northern middle latitudes.

This presentation leaves two apparent gaps, one between the strip and the polar cap, the other near the southern horizon. I have taken care of the northern gap by attaching some stars to the northern edge of the strip. In other views, I have attached them to the polar cap. I have filled the southern gap by attaching some stars to the southern edge of the strip. That southern gap, you'll recall, is the area where the remaining six first-magnitude stars at times appear when you are south of about latitude 34°.

Our strip appeared as a cylinder rather than barrel-shaped. The polar cap is printed as a disk. But that matters little. The distortion caused by these presentations is far less than on any of the visual aids you met in the preceding chapter.

I'll grant you that setting the time of night opposite a date on a star finder is simpler than looking up star time in a table, or even getting it from Polaris and Kochab. (When you recognize some star or constellation due south of you, you don't have to do either.)

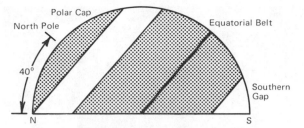

Fig. 53. Diagrammatic view of the same coverage, latitude 40°N.

But no star finder can allow for a change in latitude as easily as you can with the strip chart. You simply tilt it more or less.

There is a limit to how far this tilt is practical. Until now I have catered to observers in the belt of latitudes where most of my readers are likely to watch the night sky—roughly, the northern temperate zone: That is, north of the Tropics and south of the Arctic Circle.

But some readers of this book may live outside this belt, take a cruise, or simply be curious to know what stars people in other areas see at a given time and date.

The time/date part is easy: For a given local time and date, *star time is the same everywhere in the world.*

The latitude causes problems.

North of the Coverage Area

North of 60°N and right to the North Pole, there is no great problem with our system.

In latitude 60°N the bottom edge of the strip map will just touch your southern horizon. (Fomalhaut, when due south of you, should just kiss the horizon.) The top of the

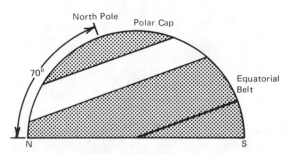

Fig. 54. Same coverage for latitude 70°N.

strip, directly above your south point, will be 30° below your zenith. (Pollux, when highest in the sky, will be three spans above your southern horizon.)

You won't have to worry in that zone about the southern first-magnitude stars. They'll never become visible. Old friends will disappear: Sirius in latitude 74°N, Antares even in latitude 64°N. (All these latitudes are theoretical limits. Atmospheric extinction will already make them look like less than first-magnitude stars a few degrees south of these limits.)

Rey's book *The Stars: A New Way to See Them* gives star maps for latitudes 60°N and 70°N for star times 0, 6, 12, and 18^h. That gives you usually one evening and one morning map during the hours of darkness for any date.

The Rude star finder has overlays for 65, 75, and 85°N.

At the North Pole, star finding becomes easy. You'll see at the same time *all* the stars in the upper half of the strip, stars north of the celestial equator. The celestial equator falls on your horizon. So this is the one place in the Northern Hemisphere where you see the strip joined in the shape of a cylinder. The stars never rise or set but just drift, at the same distance from your horizon, westward.

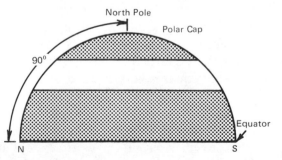

Fig. 55. Same coverage at the North Pole (latitude 90°N).

Polaris there is almost at your zenith at all times; the polar cap rotates around it, and the stars there also keep at the same distance from your horizon. Deneb, for example, whether you look for it on the strip or the polar map, will be halfway between your horizon and your zenith during all hours of the polar darkness. (That darkness by the way, lasts six months if you count the weeks of dawn and dusk.)

In the Northern Tropics

South of the coverage area of the preceding chapters, the strip rises more and more steeply, the polar cap drops lower and lower, and the southern gap becomes larger and larger.

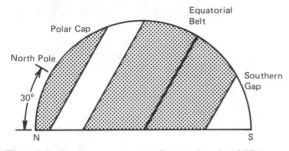

Fig. 56. Same coverage for latitude 30°N.

It's time to add an individual star map to cover that gap.

It looks very much like the map of the polar cap we have used all along. Only, instead of having the celestial North Pole for center, it is constructed around the celestial South Pole.

The relation of the *two* polar caps and the area covered by the strip map is best visualized on the equator of Earth, latitude 0°. The celestial equator here goes through your zenith. The strip is straight up and down. A star at the celestial equator—say, one of the stars in the Belt of Orion—rises in the east (as it does everywhere in the world except at the poles). But here it stays east of you as it climbs higher. Six hours after rising, it passes through your zenith, aiming for the west point on your horizon. So for the next six hours it will be continuously west of you.

Since all other stars move parallel to the

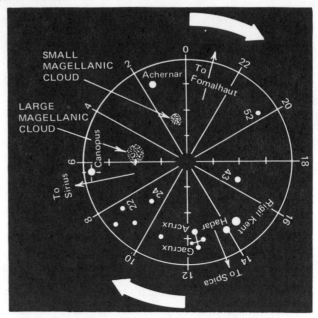

Fig. 57. Map of southernmost stars.

celestial equator, they'll all make arcs parallel to that of the star on the equator.

On the equator on Earth one half of the north polar cap is above the horizon at any one time, and so is one half of the south polar cap. (That, by the way, makes the equator the only location on Earth where in the course of one year *all* the stars become visible—at least theoretically. Practically, you will not see Polaris, or its counterpart near the celestial South Pole. Atmospheric extinction blots them out.)

To use the south polar cap on the equator, imagine it turning around the south point on

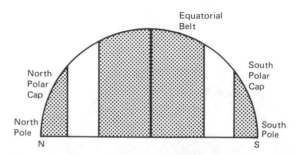

Fig. 58. Coverage of the dome of the sky by *three* star maps on the equator (latitude 0°).

your horizon (in the direction of the arrow) and align its hour of star time to match the star time used for placing the strip map.

North of the equator, the celestial South Pole will still be below your horizon (in latitude 10°N, 10 degrees below the horizon; in 20°N, 20 degrees).

You will find it difficult to measure hands and spans and fingers below the horizon to find that imaginary point, the center of the south polar cap. So, to align the map of that area for your latitude, do this. On the map, find the distance from the celestial South Pole that corresponds to your latitude. Say you are in latitude 15°N. Draw a mental circle around the pole with a diameter of 15°. (The marks on the axes in the drawing are 10 degrees apart, so your circle will pass halfway between the first and second marks from the pole.) This circle will just touch your horizon from below at the southern point of your horizon.

In Rey's book you'll find four star maps, again for star time 0, 6, 12, and 18ʰ, with horizons indicated for 30°N, 20°N, and 10°N, and four more for the same star times with horizons for 10°N, the equator, and 10°S.

On the Rude star finder you'd use the overlays for 25, 15, and 5°N.

Southern Latitudes

For someone used to watching the sky, however casually, in midnorthern latitudes, everything seems topsy-turvy south of the equator.

The sun still rises on some easterly bearing and sets in the western sky; but at noon it is not south of you but *due north*. (The sun is also north of you in the northern Tropics during part of the summer, but there that may pass unnoticed. The southernmost Bahamas, for example, are definitely in the Tropics, but you are virtually standing on your shadow. Even in Panama—latitude 9°N— where the sun in midsummer at noon is 1½

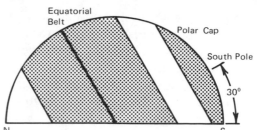

Fig. 59. Coverage by two star maps for latitude 30°S. There is now a gap in the *northern* sky.

hands from your zenith toward the north, many transplanted northerners have never noticed that strange behavior of the sun.)

Herodotus, the fifth-century B.C. historian, heard in Egypt about a fabulous voyage in the days of Pharaoh Necho (610–595 B.C.): A Phoenician fleet sailing from the Red Sea, and proceeding along the coast of Africa, had returned by the Pillars of Hercules, the Strait of Gibraltar.

Members of that epic circumnavigation— equivalent to three Atlantic crossings in distance—for the rest of their lives were considered fools or liars. Who else would try to make you believe they had seen the sun at noon in the north?

More than twenty-five hundred years later, it seems proof that they had really made that voyage. Unless he had seen the sun in the north, who'd make up such a tall tale?

The sun in the north at noon is not the only thing topsy-turvy in the Southern Hemisphere: The familiar constellations, and the moon, appear upside down.

How does that come about? When you aligned the strip map, you tilted it more and more away from your southern horizon as you traveled, say, from New York to Florida. On the equator the strip map was straight up and down. As you travel farther south, you have to tilt it some more, until what was the bottom edge in the Northern Hemisphere becomes the top edge in the Southern.

You can prove it in another way. Raise this book until it is virtually above your head. If you keep moving it farther, you won't be able to see it unless you turn in your chair. But then you'll see the print upside down. And the type that before read from left to right will now read the other way. In this same way, the sun, moon, and stars turn from east, by way of north (instead of south), to west.

That means all the planets and the fifteen brightest stars of the strip map will be displayed in the northern sky.

Turning the strip map upside down also turns all the lettering, so the strip is here redrawn for readers in the Southern Hemisphere.

You align that strip to the celestial equator as before. And you trace the celestial equator in a very similar way.

In the following instructions, the words changed from those for the Northern Hemisphere are in italics:

In southern latitudes, face *north.* The highest point of the celestial equator will be as many degrees *north* of your zenith as your latitude. (You'll find it easier to subtract your latitude from 90 degrees, and measure that distance from the *north* point of your horizon upward.)

Example: Near Buenos Aires, in latitude 35°S, you could measure 3½ hands down from the point above your head toward the north. You'll find it easier to measure 55° (90 − 35), or 5½ hands, upward from your northern horizon.

Still facing *north,* swing your outstretched arm right, back through the point just found, and left. As before, you have now traced the celestial equator, from *east* on your horizon to *west* on your horizon. As before, you align the horizontal zero line (the celestial equator) on the strip map with the line just traced.

Imagine the hour line corresponding to your star time rising straight up from the *north* point on your horizon toward your zenith. (*Example:* the 12^h line.) The line

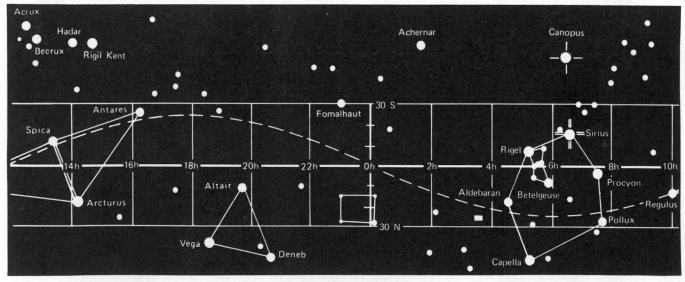

Fig. 60. Star map for stargazers in the Southern Hemisphere, including all second-magnitude stars within the strip. This strip map can be used at any star time. Most stars and hour lines appear twice on the map. To align the map with the sky, use the hour line nearest the fold. The planets Mars, Jupiter, and Saturn will never be far from the dashed curve, the ecliptic.

labeled six hours more than your star time (18^h) will slope up through the *east* point of your horizon (to your *right*). The line labeled six hours less than your star time (6^h) will slope up through the *west* point of your horizon (to your *left*).

To get a view of the southern sky from southern latitudes, do this: Turn the south polar map—Figure 57, the one with the Southern Cross—until your star time is uppermost. Then measure your latitude upward from the south point on your horizon. (Near Lima—latitude 12°S—you'd measure one hand and one finger.) That point indicates the center of the chart, the celestial South Pole.

You'll now have a gap left between the bottom edge of the strip and your northern horizon. No first-magnitude star (or planet) will ever appear there.

To fill the gap, turn the north polar map—Figure 28, the one with the Big Dipper—until your star time is uppermost. The celestial North Pole is now as many de-

grees *below* your horizon as your latitude (12° in Lima).

You may find it awkward to measure below the horizon. Instead, find the approximate distance corresponding to your latitude *above* the pole toward the numeral indicating star time. Imagine a circle drawn around the pole at that distance. (Each mark on the axes of the map is again 10 degrees.) That circle just touches your horizon at its north point.

Visual Aids for the Southern Hemisphere

Sky and Telescope magazine produces a circular star map for the Southern Hemisphere with a choice of four horizons: 10, 20, 30, and 40°S latitude. It allows for mailing delay; in the January issue you'll find the star map for early evening in February and March (star time 8^h).

Rey's book *The Stars* has four star maps (for latitudes 10, 20, and 30°S) for 0, 6, 12, and 18^h star time.

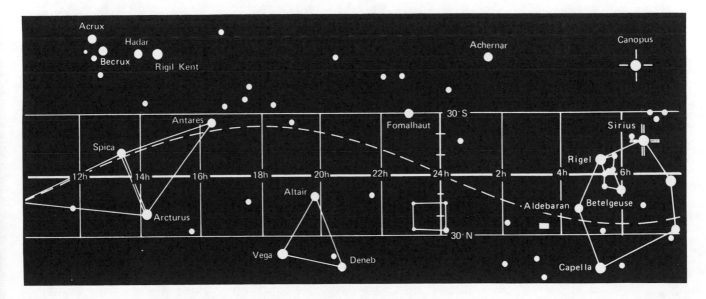

Menzel's *Field Guide* covers the Southern Hemisphere in the same manner as the Northern. (Two-hour intervals in star time, with adjustment of masks for in-between times. The masks are suitable for latitudes 5 to 45°S. In latitude 25°S, only one mask is needed for both the north and the south views.)

Besides star finders produced for a given southern latitude, such as Melbourne, Australia, the worldwide Rude star finder will help you here.

The instructions for its use in the Southern Hemisphere are simple. Turn over the star map so that the large letter *S* (rather than *N*) is on top. Then use the overlay corresponding to your latitude. Turn it so that, say, "Latitude 25°S" reads properly rather than in mirror writing. Place the overlay on the central pin of the star map. Then set the finder for star time as for the Northern Hemisphere.

PART TWO

Optical Aids for Stargazing

10

Binoculars and the Night Sky

Binoculars will greatly expand the scope of your stargazing. Of course, binoculars are not telescopes, and you won't see all the wonders astronomy books and telescope brochures show.

But modern binoculars will solve for you the question that puzzled people for thousands of years: What is the Milky Way? Like Galileo, you'll see that it is made up of millions of densely packed stars.

You'll get to see the moon, which looks pretty flat to the naked eye, as a sphere. The smudges one sees become "seas" and craters and moutain ranges.

A barely visible patch of light among the stars becomes an open cluster, a globular cluster, a nebula, or a galaxy.

Comets that are easily seen with the naked eye are rare. But with binoculars you won't have to wait a lifetime to see one.

Systematic stargazing through binoculars is good preparation for working with a telescope. One learns to find dim objects by estimating angles between reference stars and the target. And one gets introduced to some of the most popular candidates for observation—and photography—through a telescope.

Adjusting Binoculars

Perhaps you already have a pair of binoculars or can borrow one. I'm talking about true binoculars, technically known as prismatic binoculars—not mother-of-pearl opera glasses, or "field glasses," a term now reserved for the types that employ only lenses.

Prisms are a cunning way of folding a long light path into a small space. The distance from front lens to eye may be only 6 inches (15 cm). Yet the path the light travels inside the binoculars is about 15 inches (38 cm), as far as in a spyglass. In the usual prismatic binoculars, each barrel has at least fourteen optical surfaces that have to be ground, polished, and assembled to a high grade of precision.

If you have just borrowed binoculars or

have not used your own for a long time, you may be hazy about the best procedure for adjusting them to your eyes and the distance of the object you want to observe.

For all astronomical viewing, distance is what is loosely called "infinity." In this case, infinity is everything farther than, say, 100 feet (30 m). So you don't have to wait for the moon or the stars to become visible. A TV aerial, a chimney, brick wall, or tree at least 100 feet away will do nicely for the adjustment.

Two mechanisms for adjustment are in common use. You can tell them apart by a look at the eyepiece mounts. When *both* mounts have markings such as

$$2 . + . 0 . - . 2$$

you are looking at *individual-focus* binoculars.

If only *one* eyepiece mount is marked, you are holding *center-focus* binoculars. They will have a knurled wheel between the barrels that moves both eyepieces toward or away from the front lens.

Both kinds of binoculars let you spread the barrels or bring them closer together to adjust for the distance between your eyes.

Photo 4. Binoculars—the markings on the left eyepiece only and the focusing wheel between **the barrels identify them as a center-focus model. Photo: Edmund Scientific Co.**

Don't bother with that just yet. Either type is adjusted for one eye at a time first.

Here is the procedure for *individual-focus* glasses:

1. Find a suitable distant target.
2. Set both eyepieces to zero.
3. Hold a card over the right front lens and look through the left eyepiece. (You may use your palm to block the right lens if you don't touch the lens; that's bad for its coating. Don't just close one eye. That affects the focus in the other, which is the reason for using a card in eye examinations.)
4. Gradually turn the eyepiece you are looking through. If the image gets less sharp, turn the other way. When a small turn one way or the other makes the image less sharp, you have found the best setting for that eye. Note the mark on the eyepiece, so in the future you can come back to it without fiddling.
5. Block the other barrel with your card and focus the other eyepiece. Again note the marking.
6. Now look through both eyepieces at the same time and quickly adjust the spread of the barrels until you see *one* circle—not the two overlapping circles you see in the movies to indicate the captain is looking through binoculars.

Some binoculars have a scale for that setting, too; the figures may run from 60 to 80. You may also want to remember that number. But it's only the work of a second to adjust the spread for comfort.

You can save yourself the trouble of remembering the eyepiece settings by putting little triangles of tape at the correct setting.

For *center-focus* binoculars, use this procedure:

1. Find a suitable distant target.
2. Set the adjustable eyepiece to zero.

3. Hold a card over the barrel with the adjustable eyepiece. You may use your palm—with care; but don't just close the eye.
4. Look through the other barrel and turn the knurled wheel gently until the object is as sharp as possible. When turning the wheel a little in either direction makes the image worse, you have found the best adjustment.
5. Without changing the distance setting, cover the barrel you have just looked through. Now adjust the eyepiece as in step 4 for individual-focus glasses.
6. Look through both barrels at the same time until you see *one* circle, as in step 6 above.

I have not mentioned what to do if you wear eyeglasses. If you adjusted the binoculars—of either type—and took your glasses off, fine. If you left them on and had no trouble, even better; it'll save you the taking-off, putting-on routine. But sooner or later the binoculars will hit your eyeglasses and dent your nose. To buffer such collisions, some binoculars come with rubber cups on the eyepieces. You can also buy the cups separately.

Some binoculars will not let you see the whole field when your eyes are at the greater distance made necessary by your eyeglasses. To remedy that, the eyecups of some binoculars retract to let you get closer.

Choosing Binoculars

If you have a choice in what binoculars to borrow, try for a pair marked 7×50. You may wonder what these markings mean, and why these glasses are my first choice for stargazing.

The "7×" indicates power, or magnification. It simply means that these glasses make everything appear seven times larger than seen without them. That makes a bird, or the moon, seem seven times closer.

You may think, as anybody would: Let me get the greatest magnification possible. But there's a hitch, quite apart from price and magnification of optical faults: You can't hold the glasses still enough. The moon, or a bird, will jump up and down, with the result that you won't see any more detail.

Everyone seems to agree that hand-held binoculars should not exceed 8× magnification. Even where you can steady your elbows, as in stargazing, you will not get a steady image with much higher magnification. That makes zoom binoculars, in which you can change the magnification—by hand or even with a battery-powered motor—from, say, 7× to 15×, a poor choice. These glasses are also heavy and expensive, and most are beset with optical problems.

Some binoculars have a tripod socket that fits photographic tripods. Edmund Scientific Co. sells a clamping device that fits over the shaft around which the barrels swivel, and screws to a tripod.

You could make a tripod adapter yourself. In a piece of hardwood drill three holes. The middle one takes your tripod screw. Through the outer ones string a shoelace to hold the binoculars.

Mounting binoculars on a sturdy tripod works well on a mountain lookout. But it's rather awkward for observing astronomical objects where they show up best—high above the horizon.

The second figure in binocular markings, the one that follows the "×," is simply the diameter of the front lens, measured in millimeters. One inch equals about 25 mm, so the "50" in "7×50" means the front lens is almost exactly 2 inches in diameter. You can easily verify that with a ruler. On a pair of binoculars marked 7×35, you would find the diameter of the front lens—35 mm—measures about 1⅜ inches.

The larger the lens, the more light it admits, just as a larger pipe carries more water than a smaller one. Does, then, a pair of 7×50's make things look brighter than, say, a pair of compact 7×21's? The answer is strange: no in daylight, yes at night.

That calls for an explanation.

Hold a pair of binoculars at arm's length and aim them at the sky or a white wall. In each eyepiece you'll see a bright circle. You can measure the circle's diameter if you have a metric ruler. For the 7×50's you'll get 7 mm, for the 7×21's you'll measure 3 mm. (How do I know? I calculated it by dividing the second number, the front lens diameter, by the first number, which indicates magnification; 50 mm ÷ 7 gives about 7 mm; 21 mm ÷ 7 gives 3 mm.)

The circles you have just measured, or calculated, are technically known as the *exit pupils* of the binoculars. The "exit" part is clear enough: That's where the light exits. But why "pupil"? Perhaps because these spots are normally right next to the pupils of your eyes. And in that lies the strange no-yes answer.

You have noticed that in daylight everyone's pupils are small (2–3 mm); in dim light they open to about 7 mm. In bright light a binoculars' exit pupil of 3 mm fills your own pupil with light. A larger exit pupil just wastes some of its light on your iris. Result: The larger glasses don't produce a brighter image of a daylight scene or the full moon, which is amply bright.

In poor light, or nearly complete darkness, the situation is quite different. A 3 mm exit pupil lights up only part of your own pupil, which is now enlarged to about 7 mm. To make the most of existing light, you need an exit pupil of 7 mm. On the other hand, an even larger exit pupil would again spill light uselessly on your iris. So there is no point in making the front lenses of binoculars larger than seven times their magnification; hence the 7×50 glasses. For eight-power binoculars, that would work out to 8×56, but I don't believe I have ever seen such a pair.

There is yet another set of numbers on most binoculars: e.g., ''367 feet at 1000 yards.'' That describes the width of your field of vision. You would see two posts, 1,000 yards distant, if they were 367 feet apart. If they were farther apart, you'd have to shift your glasses to see them both.

Some glasses state the field width in degrees. The glasses used in the example might be labeled 7°. You can convert feet at 1,000 yards to degrees, and the other way round, by using this table:

Feet per 1,000 yards:	525	472	420	**367**	314	261
Degrees covered:	10	9	8	**7**	6	5

A 7° field is about standard for general-purpose binoculars. Glasses that cover a greater angle—wide-field or wide-angle binoculars—are sold at higher prices. The wider field is often achieved at the expense of optical perfection. For sky watching, the normal field is preferred, and a less than normal field is adequate.

Individual-focus or center-focus glasses are equally acceptable for stargazing (and for marine use, or for spotting distant game), where the focus is always the same: infinity. Individual-focus glasses are simpler to make, therefore a little less expensive; they are also easier to seal to keep dust and moisture out. For many other uses, bird watching, for example, where the focus often changes, center-focus glasses are obviously handier. (Some models focus as close as two yards or meters.)

You may be ready to buy binoculars for some reason other than looking at the night sky, and prefer the ever-popular and lighter 7×35 or perhaps 8×30, if you find you can hold them steady. You may even dream of the superb, and expensive, featherweight

roof-prism types pioneered by Zeiss and Leitz. They come in various models, such as miniature 6×20 and 8×20. All their glass surfaces are coated, while many binoculars labeled ''coated'' have only a few lens surfaces treated against light-squandering reflections.

Don't just buy a certain model because the glasses Joe lent you were good. Quality control in low- and medium-priced glasses often leaves much to be desired. Edmund Scientific's catalog states that the company tests all binoculars it buys and rejects thirty out of every hundred pairs.

You can look through glasses in the store. If they give you a headache in a couple of minutes, there's obviously something wrong with them.

You can look through the glasses from the front and spot dirt, paint dribbles, scratches, and stars. (Small bubbles in the glass are acceptable.) You can hold the glasses in their normal position, at arm's length, and look at the exit pupils. They should be perfectly round and evenly bright all the way to the edges.

For center-focus glasses, there's another quick test. Adjust the glasses for some object say 30 feet (10 m) away. Then look at a very distant object, and next at one as close as the glasses will focus. If the eyepiece needs any adjustment, the barrels are mismatched.

Other faults are harder to detect. Also, after looking through several pairs of binoculars, your eyes will refuse to notice small differences. Narrow your choice down to one or two pairs, then take a pair home with the understanding that you can bring them back for a full refund. Looking at stars is a very severe test for binoculars.

Some years ago I looked at Venus through binoculars that had showed the building across the street from the store sharp and crisp. I could clearly see the crescent shape of Venus. Then I looked at Sirius. It, too, was crescent-shaped. In fact, all bright stars looked like the moon a few days from new.

In other glasses you may find all stars tutti-frutti-colored.

If the glasses you are testing at night don't show either of these defects, pay special attention to stars near the edge of the field. Are their images—small circles—no larger than and as bright as the ones in the center? (Wide-angle glasses are especially prone to lack of this "flatness of field.")

I would stay away from oversized tripod-mounted binoculars such as 20×60's—and certainly from 30×180's, which weigh 145 pounds (66 kg)—and spend the money on a telescope.

Observing Through Binoculars

First a warning:

Never look at the sun through binoculars—you risk instant, irreversible eye damage.

You'll get the most enjoyment from skygazing if you are reclining in an adjustable lawn chair with your elbows on the armrests steadying the glasses. A small flashlight that gives a red glow, just strong enough for you to consult a star chart without destroying your night vision, is very useful.

The *Milky Way* on a moon-dark night is a great treat for the observer armed with binoculars. That ring of faint light made up of an estimated hundred thousand million stars lopsidedly circles the star sphere. A river that runs back into itself might be a better simile. The Milky Way is not uniformly two hands wide, but narrows and spreads, splits in two around islands, and in many places ends in backwaters.

When the sky is brightened by the moon or artificial lights, you won't enjoy watching the Milky Way; when the sky is dark, you won't need a star map to find it.

Its brightest areas north of the celestial equator are in the constellations Cygnus and Aquila (reference first-magnitude stars Deneb and Altair). South of the celestial equator, the brightest areas are in Scorpius (reference star Antares) and Sagittarius, the next constellation east.

But wherever in the Milky Way you aim your binoculars, you are in for a treat.

The *Magellanic Clouds* are visible only to observers in the Tropics and the Southern Hemisphere. While the Milky Way is the galaxy of our own sun, the Large and Small Magellanic Clouds are separate galaxies. By astronomical standards, they are fairly close to us. Light from them takes a mere 200,000 years to reach us. To the naked eye, the two clouds appear like detached patches of the Milky Way. And so they do in binoculars.

The *moon,* on which one can just make out lighter and darker patches with the naked eye, becomes more interesting through binoculars.

Almost everyone overestimates the size of the moon's disk. It's only about half of one degree (about one quarter of a finger's width) in diameter. Don't expect to see an enormous globe through your binoculars.

Most casual observers would point their binoculars at the moon when it is full. The view at that time is dominated by some white rays radiating from several craters. The most prominent ray system starts from Tycho (TEE-koh or TEYE-koh), near the South Pole of the moon. The rays remind one of the meridians on a terrestrial globe. Kepler (KEP-luhr) and Copernicus (koh-PUHR-ni-kuhs) also have well-developed ray systems.

The full-moon time is also good for getting an overview of the *maria* (MA-ree-uh)—plural of *mare* (MA-ray)—the waterless seas of the moon. They all seem to blend into one another except Mare Crisium (KREE-see-uhm) near the right limb of the moon. It and the crater Grimaldi (gree-MAL-dee) near the opposite extreme make good reference

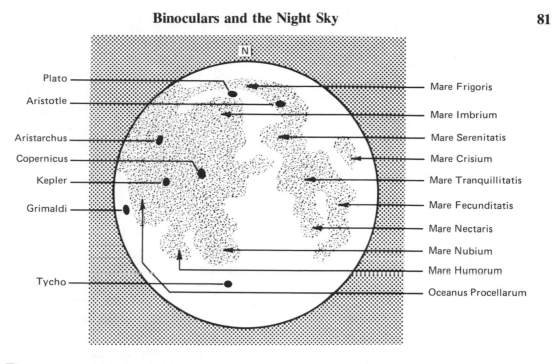

Fig. 61. The moon seen through binoculars.

points. If you have a moon map, you may find these two features reversed. Explanation: The map shows the moon as seen in a telescope, upside down. Simply turn such a map 180 degrees.

When the moon is not full, much more detail becomes visible: craters, chains of mountains, and the divisions between one mare and the next. Mountains and craters cast shadows, and the line where light and dark meet—the *terminator*—is full of ragged detail even through binoculars.

The best nights for watching that particular sky show are from five nights before first quarter to five nights after, and five nights before last quarter to five nights after. The calendar at the end of this book gives the dates of first and last quarters through 1990.

It's a spectacle well worth watching even if you don't care to learn the names of more than a few features on the moon.

Open star clusters are groups of stars moving through space together. Here are a few that are not hard to spot with binoculars. The M numbers are their designation in Messier's

catalog of nebulae and clusters. I also give their approximate right ascension and declination.

The Pleiades (M45)—3.7ʰ, N24°—in the constellation Taurus, the Bull, are the most famous of open clusters. To find Taurus, we used first-magnitude Aldebaran. The Pleiades are about 15 degrees from that star in a northwesterly direction: that is, away from the Belt of Orion (Fig. 41).

That's a good practice object for using the field of your binoculars for measuring degrees in the sky. Say your binoculars have the standard 7° field (about 367 feet at 1,000 yards). Fifteen degrees, then, is a little more than two field diameters in your glasses. Get Aldebaran into the field. Move it to the left edge of the field. Now step off one field by noting some star northwest—more or less—of Aldebaran. From that star step off another field in the same direction. A little more toward the northwest and the Pleiades should be right in view. That's a good trick to learn if you plan to use a telescope later.

The Pleiades are also known as the Seven

Sisters. Even with the best eyes, people can usually see only five or at the most six stars. Through binoculars you see many more stars there, all shrouded in a dust cloud that scatters and reflects the light from the stars within it.

The roughly circular open cluster in Canis Major, the Large Dog (M41)—6.7^h, S21°—is easily found about 4 degrees south of Sirius. That cluster is just visible to the naked eye under good conditions. It has a reddish star at its center.

The Beehive, or Praesepe (M44)—8.6^h, N20°—is located in Cancer, the Crab. (But it is *not* the famous Crab nebula [M1], which is named after its shape, is in Taurus, and requires a telescope.) The Beehive is roughly on a line from Pollux to Regulus, a little closer to Pollux—about 16 degrees away. It contains some distinctly orange stars. You may just make out this cluster with the naked eye when conditions are good.

M7 has no common name. Its coordinates—17.9^h, S35°—place it in Scorpius, the Scorpion, specifically about 4 degrees east and a little north of the scorpion's stinger. You should be able to see it with the naked eye.

Globular clusters are spherical systems of tens of thousands of stars, with the stars strongly concentrated near the center.

NGC 5139 appears as a fourth-magnitude star at 13.4^h, S47° in the constellation Centaurus, the Centaur. It has no Messier number for the simple reason that Messier, working in France, could not see it. Unless you are far enough south to have the Southern Cross well above your horizon, don't bother looking for it.

The designation NGC 5139 is astronomer's code for the number of this cluster in J. L. E. Dreyer's *New General Catalogue of Nebulae and Clusters of Stars* (1888). By the way, Johann Bayer, who in 1603 suggested the method of giving stars in any one constellation successive Greek letters—usually in order of diminishing brightness—listed this cluster as star *omega,* the last letter of the alphabet, in Centaurus.

You'll find it by going north (toward Spica) 14 degrees from the point halfway between Becrux and Hadar. An old edition of Norton's *Star Atlas* describes it as "a noble globular cluster."

M4 is a globular cluster without a common name in Scorpius, the Scorpion, at 16.3^h, S27°. It is a rather faint object, but easy to find since it is right next to Antares. Look for it less than a finger's width west of that first-magnitude star.

The Great Cluster in Hercules (M13)—16.7^h, N37°—is one of the finest of this type. The constellation Hercules itself is not easy to find. To find the cluster through binoculars, I'd start from Vega, then sweep parallel to the celestial equator westward. The cluster is more than 20 degrees from Vega, and just barely visible to the naked eye.

Other objects for binoculars must include the Great Nebula in Orion (M42)—5.5^h, S5°—a *diffuse nebula,* defined as a cloud of gas or solid particles, of irregular shape. If you have rambled through the Milky Way, you likely have already stumbled on such nebulae.

The one in Orion is easy to find: a little south of the Belt of Orion, readily visible without binoculars as part of Orion's dagger dangling from the belt.

The Andromeda Nebula (M31)—0.7^h, N41°—is a spiral nebula: that is, another galaxy, and it is one of the nearest ones, although ten times as far away as the Magellanic Clouds. To find it, locate the Square of Pegasus. Sweep with your binoculars diagonally from southwest to northeast. Continue in that direction about the length of the diagonal and you'll have M31 in your field of view. To the naked eye it appears as a small white patch.

Comets are discovered—and expected returning comets are rediscovered—through telescopes when they are still a good distance from the sun. Through binoculars—and very occasionally with the naked eye—comets become observable only shortly before they loop around the sun. Near the sun they are lost in twilight, but soon they become visible again as they speed away from the sun.

So you are most likely to see a comet before dawn in the eastern sky, or after dusk in the western—just about where you'd expect to see Mercury.

The current issue of *Sky and Telescope* or *Astronomy* may have exact positions for any bright comet. If there is a planetarium near you, its director may be able to give you that information. Should a comet become visible to the naked eye, the newspapers will report it.

If you ever locate one of these comets after a lengthy search with binoculars, you'll be surprised that afterward you can find it instantly with the naked eye.

11

Astrophotography Without a Telescope

You may have wondered if you could photograph some of the spectacles in the night sky without a telescope. You can, if you hanker for experimentation, have lots of patience, and don't get discouraged by failure.

For most night photography you'll need a camera that lets you take time exposures, that lets you attach a cable release, and that can be solidly mounted.

If your camera has not got a *T* setting, which keeps the shutter open until you press it again, you may still be in luck if it has a *B* setting. On that setting the shutter stays open as long as you press down on it. You can get a cable release that keeps the shutter open until you release a latch or screw at the hand end of the release.

If you don't see any place to attach a cable release to your camera, don't give up. Many cameras have a protective ring around the shutter button. That ring unscrews and you can get a cable release to fit in its place.

Even if close inspection of camera and in-struction book—if available—shows no way to attach a cable release, you can still use the camera if it has a *T* setting.

Use the hat trick. When ready to take the picture, open the shutter but first cover the lens with a hat. Keep the hat in place until the vibration caused by opening the shutter has died down—at least one half minute. Make your exposure by removing the hat. When the time is up, replace the hat; only then close the shutter. If you don't own a hat, use a pot.

You may find an otherwise serviceable camera with the shutter stuck wide open. Use a lens cap to keep light out of the camera until you are ready to shoot. Then, under your hat, remove the lens cap and expose. Replace the hat first, then the lens cap.

Next you'll need a *solid* tripod. The light-weight models that fit in an oversized pencil case are useless for time exposures. Much better, use a C-clamp, sold in photographic stores, meant to attach a camera to any available support. Such a clamp attached to, say, a balcony railing is steadier than most tripods.

Most cameras will have a tripod socket that fits either tripod or clamp. If your camera lacks such a fitting, you cam improvise some lash-up, perhaps from a piece of wood and some sturdy rubber bands.

You may be tempted to start your photographic experiments with some star field: say, a bright constellation. The result is likely to disappoint you. Any exposure long enough to show any but the very brightest stars will show all stars as short dashes. The length of each dash depends on two factors: the distance of the star from the celestial equator, where the motion is greatest, and the length of your exposure.

This will give you an idea of the length of the dash made by a star near the celestial equator: With a standard lens—neither wide-angle nor telephoto—in a four-minute exposure the dash will be about $1/40$ of your film width. That works for any camera from 35mm, through $2\frac{1}{4} \times 2\frac{1}{4}''$ (6×6cm), to postcard or view camera. And it works whether you measure in inches or metric units.

Perhaps the most spectacular photograph you can take makes a virtue of that nuisance: a photograph of star trails.

Near the poles—near Polaris in the Northern Hemisphere, or in the constellation Octans in the Southern—the stars barely move. The farther from the pole, the longer their trails.

If you include the pole in your photograph, all the stars will leave concentric arcs around the barely moving star nearest the pole—Polaris or Sigma in Octans. Since one revolution (360°) takes twenty-four hours, a six-hour exposure will make 90° arcs; a four-hour exposure, 60° arcs; a three-hour exposure, 45° arcs.

During such long exposures, unfortunately, the sky also registers on your film. Unless the sky is pitch-black, the sky fog will overwhelm your star trails. That restricts sky photography to periods without moonlight, and it eliminates city and many suburban locations.

You may be tempted to use the largest lens opening to record the dimmest stars. But if you have, say, an $f/2$ lens you may be wise to stop down to at least $f/3.5$ to get sharper star trails. By experiment, you may find that with a particular film you can stop down much more drastically without losing too many stars but staying ahead of the sky fog.

You can have fun experimenting with black and white or color film.

As with many other photographs, you'll get more interesting shots if you include some foreground. Silhouettes of trees or unlighted buildings, an old church for example, may nicely frame your star trails.

One thing to watch out for during your exposure is dew forming on your lens. It will spoil your picture. Wiping off the dew will almost certainly move the camera. Best advice: Start over or try again tomorrow.

Occasionally a plane will record on your film. If you see it before it enters the field of view of your camera, you can shield the lens with the hat until the plane has passed.

But these plane tracks may give you another idea. Why not record meteors?

You may accidentally catch an odd meteor. Such shooting stars occur throughout the year at the rate of a few in each hour over the entire sky. Since your camera records only a small part of the sky, chances for catching one of these *sporadics* are not good.

You can increase your chances. In any night there will be more shooting stars in the small hours of the morning than before midnight. The reason: Your part of Earth then faces in the direction of our planet's orbit around the sun, so it will catch more space debris, just as the windshield of a moving car catches more raindrops than the rear window.

At certain times of the year you'll see many more meteors during one night than normally. That happens when Earth in its orbit crosses the orbit of a comet that has left material behind—much as a truck may leak gravel along its route.

If during such a *meteor shower* you traced back each individual meteor to its origin, you'd find that all the tracks seem to radiate from one point, the *radiant*. The showers are named after the constellations in which the radiant is found: Leonids for Leo, Orionids for Orion. . . .

Some of the more productive annual meteor showers, with date of maximum yield, are listed below. Some showers build up to the maximum over a few nights and then diminish in about the same number of nights. The number of nights before and after maximum is listed in the column headed "± Days." The number of meteors—over the entire sky—per hour is given under "Rate."

SHOWER	MAXIMUM	± DAYS	RATE
Quadrantids	Jan. 3	1	40
Lyrids	Apr. 22	2	15
Aquarids	May 5	3	20
Aquarids	July 29	-	20
Perseids	Aug. 12	4	60
Orionids	Oct. 21	2	25
Taurids	Nov. 4	-	15
Leonids	Nov. 16	-	15
Geminids	Dec. 13	3	50
Ursids	Dec. 22	2	15

Unfortunately, even some of these regular showers don't always produce as expected. On the other hand, a rather poor shower may in one year be abnormally rich.

Set up your camera as close to the date of maximum as weather permits, after midnight if possible, in the dark of the moon, and as far away as you can from civilization and its sky glow.

When you see several shooting stars, aim your camera in the direction of the action and take a time exposure as for star tracks. Leave the shutter open until you think you have caught a fair number. You can then wind on the film, and take the next exposure. . . .

The American Meteor Society (AMS) has a photographic program. If you are seriously interested in continued work with the society, have access to a dark site, and have at least one camera with a *f*/2.5 or faster lens, get in touch with headquarters, enclosing a stamped, self-addressed, long envelope. The address is: American Meteor Society, Department of Physics and Astronomy, State University College, Geneseo, New York 14454.

By the way, you can join the society's program of visual observation, which needs no equipment, only grim determination to learn and stick with it. Hourly counts of meteors are easy. But another program, plotting meteor tracks, requires an intimate knowledge of the constellations.

Minimum age for active members is eighteen years (a novice must be fourteen and have parental permission). The work has to be done in unlighted, often lonely places. So young girls are discouraged unless they have a safe observing location.

This is a small group and not equipped to handle large numbers of inquiries, so don't bother them unless you are really serious.

Photography with Binoculars

You may be tempted to take photographs through your binoculars. With a lot of patience, you can take snapshots of the moon. But don't expect results to equal the views you have seen in astronomical books or magazines.

Binoculars—or for that matter a monocular, one half of a pair of binoculars—will act as a makeshift telephoto lens. You can easily calculate the effect. Seven-power binoculars in front of your regular 50 mm focal-length lens will act as a telephoto lens of 350 mm. But the quality and sharpness are likely to be poorer.

As with any long-focus lens, camera movement—even that caused by the shutter or mirror—will be magnified. A solid support is absolutely necessary.

The easiest setup is with a single-lens reflex camera. If you have, or can borrow, an SLR 35mm camera, fine. You could also use a $2\frac{1}{4} \times 2\frac{1}{4}''$ (6×6cm) single-lens reflex. I have even played with a twin-lens reflex camera of that size. But the shift from viewing lens to taking lens introduces added complications.

Whatever your camera, start with a daylight test. Set your camera to infinity and open the lens to its widest stop. Then somehow arrange one of the eyepieces of your binoculars in front of your camera lens, the two not quite touching. Focus your binoculars until the image in your viewfinder is sharp (and fills it as much as possible). Then fine-tune the alignment for sharpness from edge to edge.

You may find it quite impossible to keep alignment and distance between binoculars and camera steady, even for a test.

I suggest you breadboard it. (*Breadboarding* is originally a radio experimenter's term, meaning putting the component temporarily in place to see if a circuit will work.) Here you can literally use a breadboard. Make your binoculars comfortable by resting them on blocks of scrap wood, note pads, or whatever, on an outdoor table or other flat support. Then add shims to bring the center of the eyepiece to the level of the camera lens. If it is already too high, shim the camera.

Slide the camera into place and focus the binoculars. Examine the screen of your viewfinder critically with a magnifier. (The image may look more crisp if you can keep out most of the light between glasses and camera. Improvise a sunshade.)

When you are satisfied, you may take a test shot.

Some cameras with through-the-lens exposure meters will take into account the problems introduced by the binoculars. Other cameras will not understand what you are doing when you put binoculars in front of your lens.

Then you'll have to calculate the effect. First you multiply the power of your binoculars (7×) by the focal length of your camera lens (say, 50 mm). The result (350 mm) must be divided by the diameter of the front lens of your binoculars (say, 35 mm). That gives the effective f/stop you should use, 10 in this example. Call it f/11, the nearest commonly marked stop, and proceed to take your reading and set your shutter speed as if your camera had been stopped down to f/11, although the lens may be wide open at f/3.5.

A cable release will prevent everything from shifting during your test exposure.

To make the test more meaningful, bracket your exposure (especially if you are using color film) by taking three exposures. Vary your timing by a factor of about 4 for color. If your exposure calculation indicates $^1/_{125}$ second, take one at $^1/_{31}$, one at $^1/_{125}$, and one at $^1/_{500}$ second. For black and white film, which allows much wider latitude, you may want to vary exposures by a factor of about 8; expose, for example, at $^1/_{15}$, $^1/_{125}$, and $^1/_{1000}$.

As you wind the film between exposures, everything gets out of line, of course; even on this horizontal setup you'll have to rearrange everything.

To make it more solid, you could drill four holes through the breadboard (or any other board) and lace the shaft of the binoculars—suitably supported by blocks—to the support. Drill another hole, and secure your camera with a ¼-inch, 20-thread bolt and nut.

Next you could arrange for the whole lash-up to fit a substantial tripod. First find the center of gravity in the long direction by placing a pencil crosswise between table and assembly and moving the pencil until the board just teeters. Mark the position of the pencil on the underside of the board. Repeat the balancing act with the pencil in the fore and aft direction, and mark again. The crossing point of the lines will be at the approximate center of gravity. Drill a hole a little smaller than $\frac{1}{4}$ inch, and thread it by worrying the bolt of the tripod into it. Much more elegant is a binocular-cum-camera mount from Edmund Scientific Co., which also has a rubber light guard between eyepiece and camera lens. The current price about $20.00.

During the long exposure time that you'd need to photograph stars, they'd move. The one astronomical object that's bright enough to allow exposures short enough to make its movement unimportant is the moon.

Its image on film taken through binoculars is still disappointingly small. But if it's sharp, it can be enlarged well past the customary 3× drugstore processing.

At full moon, your through-the-lens exposure meter will give a good starting point for a series of bracketing exposures. With other meters, you might try to get a reading and calculate the f/stop as above for the sunlit scene. Or just take a wild guess, but keep careful notes so you know what was what when you see the processed results.

When you have found the best exposure (which may be between two of your bracketing shots) for the full moon, this may help you for the next tests: For a moon near first or last quarter, using the same film, multiply your exposure time by 2.5. For a small crescent moon, multiply the exposure time by 10.

These are the theoretical figures. You may have to shade them a bit to get shutter speeds marked on your camera. If one of the test exposures was right on the nose, try factors of 2 and 8.

Example: For the full moon you found $\frac{1}{125}$ second the best exposure on a certain fast film. At first or last quarter, that gives $\frac{1}{60}$ second. For a small crescent moon $\frac{1}{15}$ second, or perhaps $\frac{1}{8}$ for a very small crescent should do it.

Photo 5. Bracket for photography through binoculars. Photo: Edmund Scientific Co.

12

Astronomical Telescopes

Sooner or later every serious stargazer dreams of owning a telescope. You'll expect to find some guidance here on what telescope to get. But first let me sum up my very best advice: When the urge to buy a telescope strikes you, resist the temptation.

Don't rush to the department store and tell the salesperson you are interested in a telescope. The salesperson—an expert in cameras, typewriters, and calculators—may ask you, "How much are you intending to spend?" Or he (or she) may find that out by your reaction to the first model suggested. That is not a good basis for selection.

Also, it could be misleading. The telescope that meets your pocketbook may be displayed on a virtually useless stand. The stand that will make visual observation pleasant, and also allow you to take photographs of the night sky, may cost as much again as the displayed model, stand included.

You might be tempted to write to man-
ufacturers that advertise in astronomical magazines for their catalogs. You'll find that some manufacturers specialize in one type of telescope. They may make only refractors, or only reflectors, or perhaps a type you have never heard of before. Their brochures are enticing, but of course they don't suggest you buy another maker's model. So you may end up more bewildered than before.

Who can advise you? If there is a planetarium near you, you are sure to find someone there who's knowledgeable and willing to talk to you.

Perhaps there is an astronomy club in your town or near enough for you to attend a few meetings. There are more than two hundred such clubs in the United States and Canada, meeting perhaps once or twice a month. You probably won't find them in the telephone book, but your public library will know about the one nearest you.

You are likely also to find an astronomy

buff in the person of a high school science teacher, or on the faculty of your community college.

By all means check whatever books you can lay your hands on.

But you may want a little background knowledge so that you can ask intelligent questions and understand the answers. Here are some basics.

Types of Telescope

The earliest telescopes were *refractors*. The entering light rays are bent—refracted—by the front lens (the *objective*) to create an image near the far end of the telescope tube. A second lens, the *eyepiece* or *ocular,* then magnifies that image.

With such a telescope, Galileo (who contrary to popular opinion did *not* invent the telescope) in 1610 saw the phases of Venus, craters on the moon, and spots on the sun. He discovered the first four moons of Jupiter and reported the strange shape of Saturn. But it took another forty-five years before telescopes were improved to the point of showing the reason for the odd shape: the rings.

Galileo made several telescopes: the largest 2 inches (50 mm) in diameter, with a magnification of 33 times. It can still be seen in Florence.

Galileo's telescopes were what we now call terrestrial models. Using a negative eyepiece, they showed objects right side up. Modern astronomical telescopes use a positive eyepiece, first suggested by Kepler almost as soon as he heard about the invention of the telescope. They show images upside down. That's no hardship in astronomy. For terrestrial use, such images can be turned right side up by prisms, as in binoculars.

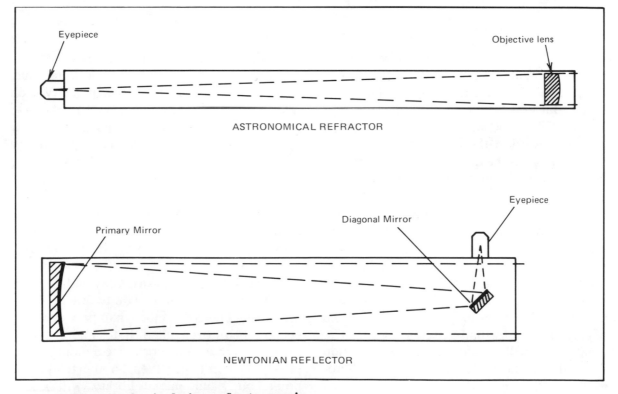

Fig. 62. The two classic designs of astronomical telescope.

Early telescopes showed bright objects surrounded by fringes of the colors of the rainbow. That defect—*chromatic aberration*—was not eliminated for more than a century. Then lenses could be made *achromatic* by joining two lenses made of different kinds of glass. Such achromats may be cemented together or held at just the right distance by thin spacers, the favored method for telescope objectives.

Reflector telescopes trace their ancestry to John Hadley, an English instrument maker.

Newton built one in 1668. His prototype is still preserved. The objective lens in front of the tube is replaced by a curved mirror at the far end of the telescope tube. The reflected image is intercepted by another mirror—flat in Newton's model—and reflected toward the magnifying eyepiece.

Newtonian reflectors—still so called—are very popular with amateur astronomers. They are free of color. They are cheaper than refractors of similar performance. A 6-inch achromatic objective lens costs more

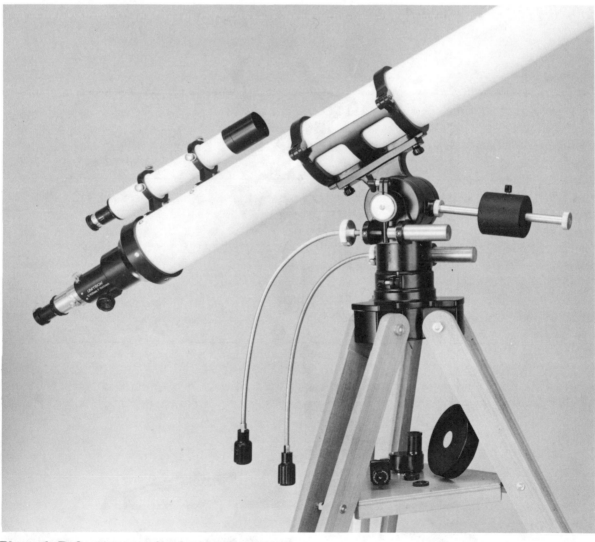

Photo 6. Refractor on tripod with altazimuth mount. Photo: Unitron Instruments Inc.

than a 6-inch reflector telescope, with mount, motor drive, eyepieces, and a few accessories thrown in.

Put differently: You get for the same price a larger telescope in a reflector.

The basic reason is this: Two pieces of nearly perfect optical glass are used in the refractor; in the reflector, the glass serves only to hold the reflective coating. In the refractor, *four* curved surfaces have to be

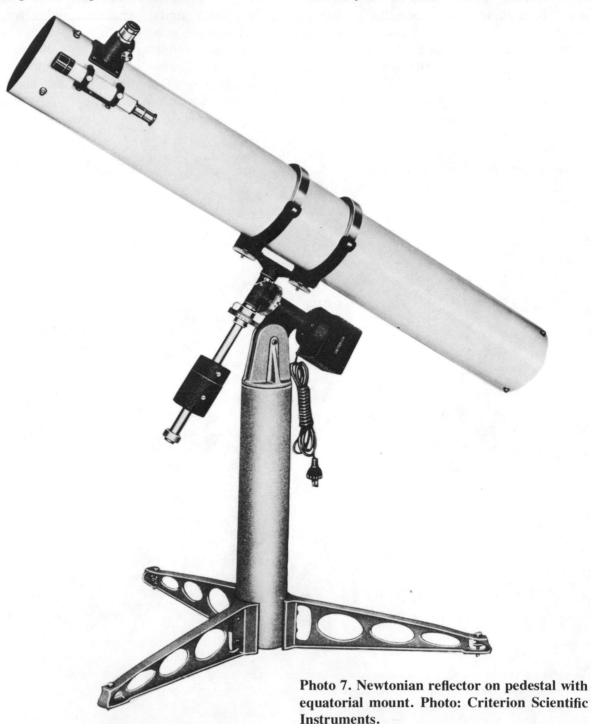

Photo 7. Newtonian reflector on pedestal with equatorial mount. Photo: Criterion Scientific Instruments.

ground and polished to close tolerances; in the reflector, only one.

A Newtonian reflector of the size you might get as a first telescope is more comfortable to use than a refractor. In the reflector, you are looking sideways into the upper end of the tube. To look straight through a refractor, you have to be underneath the eyepiece, an awkward position when you observe an object high above the horizon.

(To make such observations with a refractor more comfortable, you can get a device called a zenith prism or, more often, a *star diagonal*. The diagonal fits into the eyepiece tube and the eyepiece fits into the diagonal. A slight loss of light and degradation of the image is the price for this comfort.)

But the advantages are not all with the reflector. If they were, refractor manufacturers would have given up or switched to making reflectors.

Here are the drawbacks of Newtonian reflectors:

The mirror, a thin metallic coating on the *front* surface of a curved piece of glass, is more delicate than the glass surfaces of lenses. Dew with some salts in the atmosphere attacks the reflecting surface. You may have to have the mirror "resilvered" after a few years. (It's still called silvering, although the metal used is aluminum or

Photo 8. Star diagonal (zenith prism) brings view to more convenient position. Photo: Edmund Scientific Co.

something more exotic.) All modern mirrors are overcoated to protect the reflecting layer underneath.

The two mirrors and the eyepiece have to be accurately aligned. They probably were at the factory. By the time the reflector has been shipped to you the alignment may already be off; a refractor is more likely to arrive in mint condition. But to realign the mirrors, once you have absorbed the instructions, takes only a few minutes and requires nothing more than a light touch with a screwdriver.

You may have to realign the mirrors every time your reflector has been severely jarred. But checking whether that is necessary takes only an experienced look down the barrel. You'll soon get into the habit of checking the alignment before every observing session.

The most serious drawback of the reflector is the fact that its tube is open at one end. That causes air currents inside the tube until outside air, the tube, and everything in it is at the same temperature. These tube currents, which in theory the light rays have to traverse twice—on the way to the mirror, and between the primary mirror and the flat and eyepiece—affect the steadiness and sharpness of the image.

In practice, it is not as bad as it sounds. The air currents have been found mainly to spiral along the tube wall, outside the optical path of the light rays.

Some years ago the refractor and the Newtonian reflector were the only telescopes you had to choose from. By that time most professional work was done not by direct observation but by photography.

In 1931 Bernhard V. Schmidt, an Estonian optician, invented a sky camera—the 48-inch one at Mount Palomar is its best-known example—that led to a new type of telescope for nonprofessional stargazers.

In the Newtonian reflector, the mirror has to be parabolic. In practice, the glass later to be silvered is first ground to a perfect spherical shape. That shape is comparatively easy to make and check. Then, in a critical hand operation, the center of the mirror is deepened just enough to change the hollow sphere into a parabolic shape.

In a typical 6-inch reflector the surface of the spherical mirror is only about $1/20$ inch (1.25 mm) deeper in the center than at the edge. To make the mirror parabolic, another $1/80,000$ inch ($3/10,000$ mm) of glass has to be removed from the center, less the farther out you go from the center, tapering to zero at the edge. And that shape should be accurate to 2 millionths of an inch (0.00005 mm).

In the Schmidt design, the mirror is left spherical. A thin lens, the corrector plate, at the mouth of the tube takes the place of parabolizing the mirror.

One could mount a flat mirror—as in the Newtonian reflector—near the corrector plate and observe from the side. More commonly, another design is used. It was invented by Cassegrain in Newton's time. Cassegrain drilled a hole in the mirror and used a curved mirror where Newton placed the flat one. Result: straight-through seeing as in a refractor, a long light path in a short tube.

In a Schmidt-Cassegrain the secondary mirror is often attached directly to the corrector plate. Several manufacturers now produce that design. The corrector plate suppresses tube currents, protects the mirrors from dew and dust, and probably makes the instrument hold its adjustment better than a Newtonian. The Cassegrain design here makes for a very portable instrument and lends itself to simple mounting, as you'll see in the next chapter.

But the corrector plate in a Schmidt telescope has to be ground to a complex—hence costly—shape.

That has been overcome by a design invented in 1944 by Albert Bouwers in Holland and Dimitri Maksutov in Russia. It is generally called Maksutov.

In that design, all optical surfaces are spherical. Maksutovs have been built on the lines of Newtonian reflectors, but they lend themselves admirably to the Cassegrain design. The corrector lens is thicker than in Schmidt telescopes and easily supports the secondary mirror.

In one particularly elegant design a spot in the center of the rear surface of the corrector lens is aluminized and acts as the secondary mirror. (The Questars, by many considered the Cadillacs of small telescopes, use that design.)

Some advanced amateurs have built superb Maksutovs, and I would not be surprised if stock models at affordable prices should soon appear on the market. The cost of optical glass for the corrector lens would

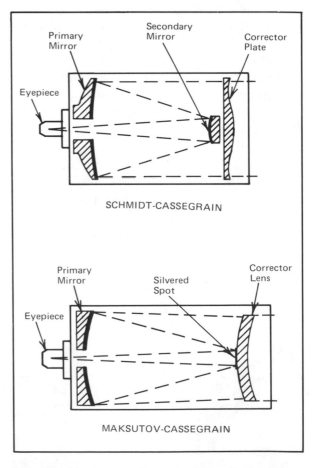

Fig. 63. The two modern designs of astronomical telescope.

**Photo 9. Schmidt-Cassegrain telescope. Note
mount for secondary mirror in center of correction plate. Photo: Celestron International.**

Photo 10. Maksutov-Cassegrain telescope.
Photo: Questar Corp.

be offset by the utter simplicity of manufacture.

The last two designs, the Schmidt and Maksutov, are known as *catadioptric* telescopes, which means that they combine a mirror (as in a reflector) and a lens (as in a refractor) in the light-gathering and focusing function.

Many of the currently available stock models are not restricted to focusing at infinity (as in astronomical use) but can be used to watch or photograph birds, game, or whatever you wish. That feature and their light weight—somewhere between the weights of portable manual and electric typewriters—have contributed to their popularity. Birds by day and stars by night!

To sum up, you now have a choice of three types of stock telescopes: *refractors* in which the primary image is formed by a (color-corrected) lens; *reflectors*—almost exclusively of the Newtonian type—where the primary image is formed by a (parabolic) mirror; and *catadioptric models*—of Schmidt or Maksutov design—in which a *spherical mirror and* a lens produce the primary image.

The catadioptric designs typically use Cassegrain design: a hole in the center of the mirror through which you observe—straight through, as in a refractor. (In the Newtonian reflector, you observe from the side, near the sky end of the tube.)

In all three designs, the primary image is enlarged in the eyepiece in the same manner.

All three types are described by their *clear aperture*. A 6-inch (150 mm) refractor has a front lens of that diameter; a 6-inch reflector has a mirror of that diameter; and a 6-inch Schmidt or Maksutov has a corrector plate or lens of that diameter. (The Mount Palomar Schmidt may be referred to as a 48–72-inch instrument. It has a corrector plate of 48-inch and a mirror of 72-inch diameter.)

This one measurement is all-important. It describes the *light-gathering power,* which controls down to what magnitude stars it will show. It also sets the limit for *resolution,* the finest detail you may see—how small a crater on the moon, or the closest double stars you'll be able to separate. And, as you will read shortly, it also limits the maximum useful magnification.

It is obvious that a larger opening admits more light. And, from elementary geometry, you may recall that the area of a circle increases with the square of the diameter—that is, the diameter multiplied by itself. *Example:* The area of a 6-inch-diameter circle is

not just twice as large as that of a 3-inch circle, but four times.

The diameter of the pupil of your fully dark-adapted eye is about ⅓ inch (8 mm). Some manufacturers give the *light grasp* of their instruments compared to that of the unaided eye. Do they use simply the geometric relation of diameters or do they make allowance for the light loss at every optical surface? Do they subtract the obstruction of the secondary mirror—typically 15 to 20 percent of the area of Newtonian and Cassegrain telescopes? Before you compare different manufacturer's figures, you had better make sure they are based on the same computing method.

The dimmest stars you can expect to see in telescopes of different clear opening is about as follows:

| DIAMETER | | STARS TO |
inches	mm	MAGNITUDE
3	75	11½
4	100	12
5	125	12½
6	150	13
8	200	13½

The naked eye cannot separate two stars that are less than 8 seconds of arc apart. How close can stars be and still show as two in a first-rate telescope on a night of average seeing? That figure, known as the Dawes limit, after William R. Dawes, an English astronomer of the last century, works out as follows for the typical telescopes considered here:

| DIAMETER | | SEPARATION |
inches	mm	seconds arc
3	75	1.52
4	100	1.14
5	125	0.91
6	150	0.76
8	200	0.57

It is to these figures the manufacturers

refer when they guarantee their optics to the Dawes limit.

The separation of double stars is given in star atlases, so you can test your own instrument. On many nights, because of atmospheric conditions, you will not reach the Dawes limit with the best optics. On a few rare nights you'll separate stars closer than the limit.

Experts in these matters agree that for the serious amateur a 6-inch reflector is the smallest size to get. For refractors, the same authorities recommend a minimum size of 3 inches. The original Questar is a 3½-inch instrument, later joined by a 7-inch of the same design. Schmidt-Cassegrains of different manufacturers start at 5 and 6 inches, with their 8-inch models not all that much more expensive.

You'll often see used telescopes advertised in astronomy magazines. And every astronomy club has members ready to go on to larger instruments as soon as they have disposed of their present ones.

You can also build a first-rate 6-inch reflector yourself. The parts and instructions are readily available. The only time-consuming operation is the grinding of the main mirror. It helps to have an expert start you off, but many rank beginners have done it just from books. The blank of Pyrex glass has two flat surfaces. If you ruin the first surface, you turn the blank over and work the other one.

After grinding, polishing, and checking you'll send your handiwork out to be silvered. (You will even see advertisements for "refiguring"—that is, correcting mistakes—at reasonable cost.)

Eyepieces

You already know this: The eyepiece magnifies the image that has been formed by the primary optics. The primary is the front lens in a refractor, the primary mirror in a reflector, or the corrector lens and primary mirror in a catadioptric telescope.

The same eyepieces can be used on a refractor, a reflector, a Schmidt, or a Maksutov telescope.

Mercifully, the outside diameter of the eyepiece mounts has been standardized. The most common diameter is 1¼-inch. In Japanese telescopes, you may find .966-inch (24.5 mm). Larger telescopes may use 2-inch eyepieces. Readily available, inexpensive adapters permit interchange of eyepieces of different outside diameters.

Since the same eyepiece used on different telescopes gives different magnifications, eyepieces are usually not labeled for magnification. (*Exception:* A set of eyepieces supplied with a given telescope may be so marked: 50×, for example.) The label gives the *focal length,* usually in millimeters.

To calculate the magnification you'll get with any given eyepiece on a given telescope, use this basic formula:

The *magnification* of the combination equals the focal length of the primary divided by the focal length of the eyepiece.

(Both measurements must be in the same units, both in inches or both in millimeters.)

> EXAMPLES:
> Focal length of primary (objective lens, mirror, or catadioptric combination) 40 inches; eyepiece focal length ½ inch. The magnification will be 80×.
> Focal length of primary 1000 mm; eyepiece focal length 12.5 mm. The magnification will be 80×.

For the *conversion* of inches and millimeters, use this approximate formula: To get millimeters, multiply inches by 25. To get inches, divide millimeters by 25. (Note: 1 centimeter equals 10 millimeters.)

> EXAMPLES:
> 40 inches equals (close enough) 1000 mm; 12.5 mm equals ½ inch.

To find the focal length of the primary when its diameter and *f*/number are given, use the next formula. The focal ratio, *f*/ratio, or *f*/number—familiar from photography—is the focal length of a lens (or mirror) divided by its diameter. That gives this formula:

The *focal length* of the primary equals its diameter multiplied by its *f*/number. (When the diameter is given in inches, you get the focal length in inches; when it's given in millimeters, you get the focal length in millimeters.)

EXAMPLES:

A 6-inch reflector is listed as *f*/8. The focal length of the mirror is 48 inches.
A 3-inch refractor is listed as *f*/15. The focal length of the objective is 45 inches.
A 100 mm telescope is listed as *f*/16. Its focal length is 1600 mm.

You may think the greater the magnification, the better. And you may be surprised that for any given diameter of the primary there is a maximum useful magnification. Above that you don't see more, you see less detail.

Take a magnifying glass and look at a photograph reproduced in a newspaper or magazine. Instead of seeing hidden detail you see a lot of dots.

You may object that the sky is not a printed picture. But the situation is similar. A star should show in a telescope as a very, very small dot. By the laws of optics it appears as a tiny disk. (The larger the objective lens or mirror, the smaller the disk becomes.) Two craterlets on the moon or a double star well beyond the Dawes limit will appear as *one* disk in your telescope. No amount of magnification will make it into two separate images.

The maximum useful magnification is generally agreed to be about 50 times the diameter of the primary in inches (300× for a 6-inch reflector). That works out to twice the diameter of the primary in millimeters (200× for a 100 mm refractor). On exceptional nights you may be able to use 60 times the diameter in inches, 2.4 times the diameter in millimeters.

That gives you the most powerful—shortest focal length—eyepiece you'll need.

Most of the time, for the moon and planets for instance, you'll be using lower magnification. Finally, you'll need a fairly-low-magnification eyepiece for extended objects such as a comet or large nebula. (Other things being equal, the field of view shrinks with increased magnification.)

Before you start calculating what magnification—that is, focal length—eyepieces you'll need, you should know about a magic device known as a Barlow. A Barlow lens slipped in front of any eyepiece about doubles its magnification. In a good, achromatic Barlow, coated on all surfaces, the loss of light and definition is tolerable.

So, by choosing three eyepieces carefully, you can get five, or six, different magnifications depending upon whether you use the Barlow or not.

If your telescope comes with a set of eyepieces, the manufacturer has made the choice for you. If you are lucky enough to meet with an astronomy club, you'll soon find out what eyepieces experienced members use for the size of instrument you are interested in.

There is a widely circulated rule of thumb for small telescopes:

EYEPIECE FOR	MAGNIFICATION	
	Diameter in inches times	Diameter in mm times
Low power, wide field	8–10	0.3–0.4
Moderate power	25–30	1.0–1.2
High power	50–60	2.0–2.4

EXAMPLES:

For a 3-inch (75 mm) refractor, that gives magnifications of 24–30×, 75–90×, and 150–180×.

For a 6-inch (150 mm) reflector, that gives 48–60×, 150–180×, and 300–360×.

Some experts give reflectors about one third lower factors than the figures given here, but agree on these figures for refractors.

There is a bewildering number of eyepiece designs. Some manufacturers, to keep the price of the complete telescope package down, supply rather poor eyepieces. If you suspect that poor imagery in your telescope—checked for alignment—may be due to that cause, borrow some first-class eyepieces before you send off for better ones.

Before you buy *any* eyepiece, try to get some expert's advice. There is not one best design, regardless of price.

In the low powers, you'll want the image to be sharp all the way from the center to the edges, all over the rather wide field. An *Erfle* may be your choice. *Orthoscopic* eyepieces—the Brandon is such a design—are widely considered best for medium magnifications.

Orthoscopics, like the Erfle and many other designs, are plagued by "ghosts": A bright star has a spurious companion evoked by internal reflections.

Triplets, or monocentric eyepieces consisting of three lenses cemented together, are free from that annoyance. They are expensive, but you may wish to choose one for your highest magnification.

Don't stick eyepieces in your pocket, but keep them each in a separate container. Remove dust from the lens surfaces only with a soft, damp artist's brush.

13

Telescope Stands, Mounts, Drives, Etc.

The purpose of a telescope stand is to get the telescope off the ground so that you can tilt it at any angle—from near the horizon to the zenith—and look into the eyepiece. Every slightest vibration of this support is magnified in your eyepiece. When you use a moderate 125× magnification, you'll see a movement of $1/1000$ of an inch in your stand as a jump of $1/8$ inch. So the support must be rock-steady.

For a permanent installation, you can dig a hole in the ground, place an upright pipe—threaded at the upper end—in it, then fill the excavation with concrete. The hole should be at least two feet (60 cm) square and, if possible, reach solid rock. Four-inch (10 cm) pipe is recommended. You may fill the pipe with concrete as well, but protect the threads while pouring it. When you get the pipe, also get *two* pipe caps. One will serve to attach the telescope mounting; the other protects the pipe thread when the telescope is stored. Some wired reinforcing rods or mesh will keep your concrete base from cracking. To avoid the chore of mixing cement and sand, you can buy instant concrete in sacks in any building supply house. Just add water.

You may not have a suitable piece of land for a permanent pier like this. "Suitable" here includes freedom from obstructions such as buildings and trees, and absence of lights. For lack of suitable land, and for other reasons, many telescopes are used on portable stands.

The most obvious solution is a tripod. Unfortunately, many tripods are wobbly affairs—the more adjustments they have, the wobblier. Sturdy tripods are costly. So many telescopes are mounted on medium-heavy tripods steadied by a shelf, braces, or tensioned wires.

A better stand, still portable and cheaper than a sturdy tripod, is a pedestal (see Photo 7). In commercial models the legs can be taken off in a few minutes with a wrench.

Then everything fits easily into the trunk of your car. Many craftsmen have built their own pedestals from pipe and lumber.

Mounts

Now you have a stand. Next you'll need, at the top of the stand, some mount that will let you aim the telescope at any point in the sky and follow the motion of the sky without effort.

The simplest mount is the *altazimuth* mount. It lets you tilt the telescope in altitude—that is, from horizon to zenith—and lets you turn it for azimuth (bearing), north, east, west, or south, or anywhere in between. Photo 9 shows a telescope so mounted. With the base horizontal, resting perhaps on a pillar, you can hit any spot in the sky as with a swivel gun.

An altazimuth mount is fine for watching still objects, such as the landscape from a mountaintop. But nothing in the sky stands still. So for astronomical work you won't be happy for long with an altazimuth mount. You must constantly reaim your telescope, then wait until the vibrations die down. By that time, your object is again about to leave your field of vision.

Sooner rather than later you will want a more sophisticated setup, known as an *equatorial* mount.

The term *equatorial* refers of course to the celestial equator, the reference line you have become familiar with since the very beginning of this book.

The stars all seem to move parallel to the equator. That's what makes sliding the strip chart for star time work. On the equator the stars move 1½ hands westward per hour. The farther a star is from the equator—the greater its declination north or south—the more slowly it moves. That's very apparent in the polar cap, where the outer stars move noticeably while Polaris, almost 90 degrees from the equator, seems to stand still. The sun, moon, and planets do change their ap-

parent distance from the equator, their declination. But in a few minutes that movement doesn't amount to much.

That gives a mount based on the equator a great advantage over one based on your horizon, as the altazimuth mount is. Once you have your telescope set up properly and aimed at a celestial object, you can follow that object by simply turning the telescope without having to raise or lower it as you would have to in an altazimuth mount.

Better yet: You can attach an electric motor, geared down to the rate of the earth's revolution, to your telescope. With such a *clock drive,* a star will seem to stand still in your field of view. You could let the machine run during the day, and if it was absolutely accurate, the same star would be at the same spot of your field when it got dark again.

Best of all, perhaps, is this: You can attach two dials to your equatorial mount of your telescope. Then you can set your telescope to the right ascension and declination from a book. Now look through the telescope: The star or planet will be in your field of view. (In an altazimuth mount you can have dials, too, but the conversion of RA and DEC into altitude and azimuth is a messy problem in spherical trigonometry.)

Basically, an equatorial mount is simply a correctly tilted altazimuth mount. You can see that by comparing the photographs of the same instrument mounted as an altazimuth and equatorially (Photos 9 and 11).

When the angle and the direction of your equatorial mount are properly set, the tilted axis points directly to the pole, hence the name *polar axis*. If you set the declination to zero (corresponding to having the telescope tube horizontal in the altazimuth position) and turn the instrument from east to west, you'll sweep out the celestial equator as you did with your arm for naked-eye observation. The dial that indicates how far you have moved the assembly is the *right ascension dial*.

When you now raise or lower the barrel,

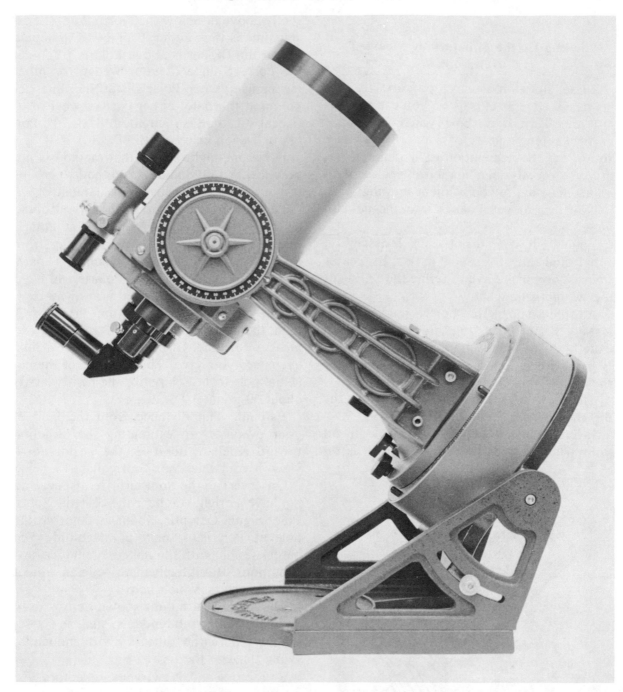

Photo 11. Schmidt-Cassegrain telescope mounted equatorially. The wedge below the base, which contains the drive motor, is ad-justed for the latitude of the observer. Photo: Celestron International.

the other dial will indicate the declination—distance north or south of the celestial equator. That's the *declination dial*. (In the altazimuth setup it would measure your star's altitude.) The shaft around which that movement takes place is the *declination axis*.

Setting Up the Equatorially Mounted Telescope

To set up such a telescope correctly, adjust the wedge as closely as you can to your latitude. Turn it as best you can to face north, keeping one leg of your tripod or pier south. Set the declination to 90 degrees, put in your lowest-magnification eyepiece (with a star diagonal for convenient viewing).

Now try to get Polaris into the field of view.

You may have to turn the whole assembly, stand and all, to see Polaris. To center Polaris, you may have to refine the setting of the wedge somewhat.

All that assumes that Polaris marks the celestial North Pole, that its declination is exactly 90°. Actually, in 1980 its declination is 5/6 of a degree less, increasing slightly for the rest of this century.

There are several methods to allow for the distance between Polaris and the pole.

In a fixed installation, for instance, you get your true north setting when Polaris is di-

rectly above or below the North Pole. (Local star time is then about 2^h or 14^h; Cassiopeia or the Big Dipper is above Polaris.) You get the correct angle of your wedge (or other mechanism) when Polaris is at the same elevation at the pole, either east or west of it. (Local star time is then about 8^h or 20^h; Pollux or Deneb bears south of you.)

For a one-night stand, that method is not practical. You'll find other methods, perhaps in your telescope instruction manual.

Failing a more exact method, you could try this: Aim your telescope not at Polaris but at a point visually one half finger from Polaris in the direction of Kochab. (That's the star about as bright as Polaris and eight fingers of your outstretched arm away from it—the only star that bright and that close.)

In the next chapter you'll read how to measure distances from the field of various eyepieces you have. The distance of the celestial pole from Polaris for the next years is about 50 minutes (5/6 degree).

Estimate that distance from the field of your eyepiece. In estimating the direction toward Kochab, don't let the upside-down view in your telescope fool you.

Observers in the Southern Hemisphere do not have a bright star near the celestial South Pole. Sigma Octantis, about as far from the pole as Polaris, is only of magnitude 5.5, barely visible with the naked eye under best conditions. But it happens to be in an area of very few stars, which helps.

The equatorial mount shown here is used mainly on short-tube models, such as Cassegrains, where the tube is short enough to swing through the fork.

Refractors and Newtonian reflectors use other variations of the equatorial mount, most often what's called a German mount. Again there are two axes, one pointing to the pole (polar axis), the other—at right angles to the first—the declination axis (Fig. 65). To show the construction, the telescope is shown in the top position.

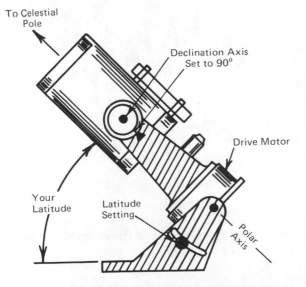

Fig. 64. Aligning a short-barreled telescope to the celestial pole. In the Northern Hemisphere, north would be at the left.

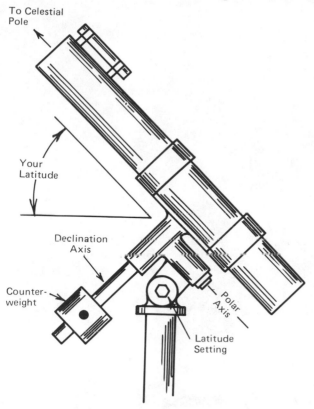

Fig. 65. Aligning a telescope in a German mount to the celestial pole. In the Northern Hemisphere, north would be at the left.

In practice, you'll be using it flopped either to the east of the pier, or, to reach other parts of the sky, west of the pier. It takes some practice to anticipate when the tube will hit the pier or tripod leg, and to roll over from east to west. Practice it in daylight until you can do it in the dark. That's where you'll have to do it.

Regardless of the variation of equatorial mounts, the right ascension dial is always centered on the polar axis, the declination dial on the declination axis.

The declination dial is fixed (except for provision for readjustment), while the RA dial is made to slip easily. Here's why. You can dispense with all calculations of star time and allowing for your longitude. Just aim your telescope at a star you know, look up

its RA, and set the dial to the figure found. To find another star, nebula, or whatever, for which you know RA and DEC, you simply turn the instrument until the two dials read correctly.

The least expensive source of that information is Edmund's *Mag 5 Star Atlas* (Edmund Scientific Co.), a 36-page paperback. It shows stars, as the name implies, down to fifth magnitude, and lists stars to magnitude 2.8, nebulae, and so on. It has a rough map of the moon and explains the use of setting circles—the RA and DEC dials—in detail.

In the same league is Terrence Dickinson and Sam Brown's *The Edmund Sky Guide*, by the same publisher.

You will find many hints on telescope, stands, mounts, and so on, including information on building them yourself, in a series

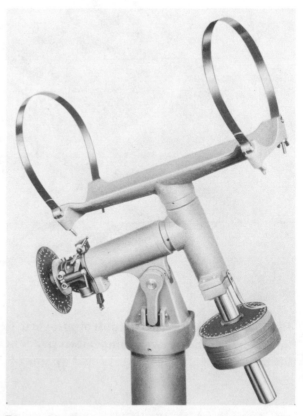

Photo 12. Equatorial mount—note setting circles. Photo: Edmund Scientific Co.

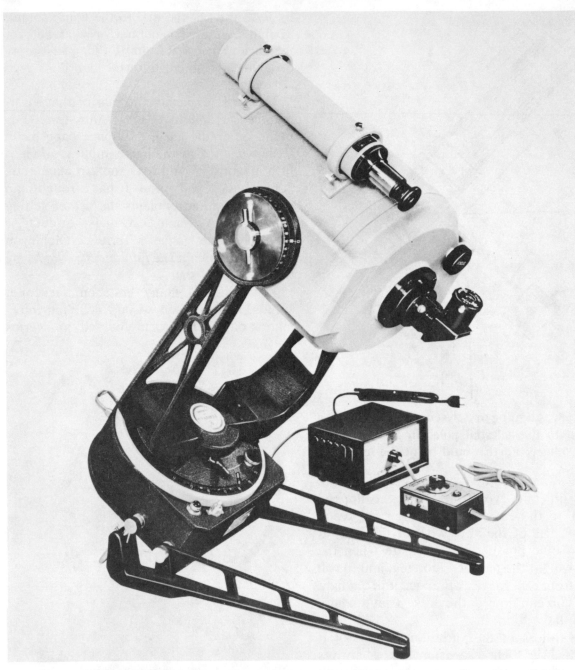

Photo 13. Variable speed control attached to another Schmidt-Cassegrain telescope. The latitude-adjuster legs convert this Dynamax to an equatorial telescope for tabletop use. Photo: Criterion Scientific Instruments.

of pamphlets by Sam Brown. They are also collected in book form—soft or hard cover—in his *All About Telescopes* (Edmund Scientific Co.).

By far the most popular star atlas is Norton's *Star Atlas* (Sky Publishing Corp.). First published in 1910, it has gone through more than a dozen editions and many reprintings.

Besides star maps with listings of interesting objects in the area of each map, and a detailed map of the moon, it has more than 100 large pages of tables and text. They range from lofty theory to homely advice on how to ease stiff drawtubes.

Another star atlas much used by advanced amateurs is A. Becvar's *Atlas Coeli Skalnate Pleso* (Sky Publishing Corp.), which shows stars down to about magnitude 7.5. It comes in two editions: bound and (handier and cheaper) as loose maps. You can mount them yourself on cardboard for use near the telescope.

The stars slowly change their right ascension and declination, mainly due to precession, the shift in the direction in which the earth's axis points. Precession affects stars in different parts of the sky differently. But the total effect, except near the poles, is small. In ten years the right ascension changes less than one minute of time for stars near the celestial equator and less than two minutes for stars in declination 80°N or S. In ten years the declination changes about three minutes of arc for the most affected stars.

Neighboring stars show virtually the same change, so star maps remain usable for long periods. Currently most such maps are drawn for 1950. Eventually they will be replaced by maps for "Epoch 2000."

A clock drive is a great convenience for visual observations and a necessity for almost all sky photography.

The motor runs on house current, your car battery, or either. It normally drives through a clutch, which allows you to fine-adjust your aim without disengaging the motor.

The motor is supposed to be designed to turn the telescope at the rate of rotation of the earth: that is, one turn in every twenty-four hours of *star* time. Even if it were, you'd have to adjust manually for the sun, which lags about four minutes a day behind the stars, the planets, and especially the moon.

There is now a magic box that allows you to run the same drive at slightly differing speeds at the turn of a switch.

Observers in the Southern Hemisphere must order a drive that runs the opposite way to the one in the Northern Hemisphere. (They also need a right ascension dial on which the numbers run in the opposite direction.)

14

Observing with a Telescope:
The Solar System

To enjoy the wonders you can see in a telescope, you have to be moderately comfortable. I'm not referring just to down jackets, thermal underwear, and mosquito dope.

Your telescope stand must be of the right height: higher for a refractor than for a Newtonian, where you observe from the other end of the tube. Steps are a great help. You may sit on them for viewing through a refractor or Cassegrain, stand on them for a Newtonian pointed high in the sky.

A flashlight—with a red lens or bulb so it won't spoil your night vision—will let you consult your atlas and read the scales.

Many observers like a *finder,* a small telescope of low magnification mounted parallel to the axis of the main scope. It saves using a low-power eyepiece to find an object, then switching to higher magnification. Other observers get along without a finder. They sight along the tube on some naked-eye stars. Some build a simple gunsight to make that easier.

An eyepiece with lighted cross hairs for finder and main scope is a convenience. It makes checking—and adjusting—the parallelism between finder and telescope easier. Many finder scopes need a star diagonal for comfortable use.

It is frustrating to have to interrupt observation because of dew forming on your object lens, corrector, or flat mirror of a Newtonian. A dew cap, a cylinder that lengthens the tube, is standard equipment. The dew caps supplied with many instruments are too short to do the job, but it's an easy matter to make one yourself. Line its inside with some dull black material. By the way: Never wipe the dew off an optical surface. Warm the surface slightly and the dew will disappear; your hand held near it will do it.

In the beginning you'll waste a lot of time hunting for dim objects, especially if your telescope mount lacks dials. Here is a technique that'll save you time: Find once and for all the width of your field of view with a given eyepiece, and use that as a celestial yardstick.

The greater the magnification—that is, the shorter the focal length of an eyepiece in a given telescope—the narrower is the apparent field. Start with your lowest-power eyepiece, the one you'll use for most of your hunting.

Aim your telescope at a star near the celestial equator. Without setting circles, use the method for finding that line for naked-eye observation. Or find a star close to the celestial equator in a constellation you already recognize, say Orion. With setting circles, set the declination to zero, and use any star now in the field of view.

Center the star vertically, then bring it to the eastern edge of the field. (In the upside-down view, that'll be the right edge.) Look at the second hand of your watch. Don't start the motor drive. Don't touch the telescope at all. Just let the star drift across the center of the field. When it reaches the western edge, mark the time again.

> Divide the seconds elapsed by 4. That gives the diameter of the field with this eyepiece in minutes of arc (').

> EXAMPLE: You found the time exactly 2 minutes, or 120 seconds. Divide by 4. Your field with this eyepiece is 30', about the diameter of the moon, or since there are 60' in a degree, about $\frac{1}{2}°$.

That knowledge will help you find a nebula one degree north from some other object. It will also help you to identify positively a cluster 30' wide.

Higher-power eyepieces will have smaller fields. In a 6-inch reflector with 180× magnification, an equatorial star may take 52 seconds to cross your field. The field then is 13' wide, not quite $\frac{1}{4}°$.

Finders have much larger fields. You can simplify the mathematics by taking the elapsed time in *minutes*. Divide that by 4, and you get the field in *degrees*.

EXAMPLE: Time from edge to edge through the center of the finder for an equatorial star is 24 minutes. Your field is 6 degrees across.

You can use that for stepping off large distances, as you did with binoculars.

Seeing

Most people are surprised that they have to learn to see through a telescope. It's not just a matter of focusing sharply. You have to learn just how far from the eyepiece your eye should be. (And if at all possible you should learn to keep the other eye open, to avoid strain.)

Veteran observers looking through the same telescope see things the beginner doesn't see. It's not unlike the city dweller looking at a hillside. He sees grass and trees, a few rocks perhaps. On the same hill a hunter sees a buck and two does; a rancher counts twenty head of cattle.

The veteran observer also has a trick: *averted vision*. The most sensitive part of your retina is not directly in your line of vision. The expert has trained himself to look a little sideways at faint objects to bring the telescopic image on the most sensitive area of his retina.

"Seeing" is also used in a different sense in astronomy.

A man I know got a small telescope for Christmas. He assembled the stand according to the directions, then set it up near an open window, and put in the eyepiece marked 300×. The next day he returned the telescope to the store. "That thing is no good. Everything hops around and is all blurred."

The warm air escaping the house, or the cold air coming in, made everything boil. The excessive magnification just enlarged the effect.

But even out of doors, most of the time there are updrafts and downdrafts that disturb the temperature distribution in the atmosphere and ruin our fun at the telescope. It's the same effect you observe over hot pavement: The distant landscape dances.

The turbulence is always worst near the horizon, least near the zenith. It changes from season to season, from night to night, and often from minute to minute.

To describe the conditions, several scales are in use. The simplest is the scale named after Eugène Antoniadi, a French astronomer, who painstakingly mapped Mars. The Antoniadi scale runs from I (perfect) to V (atrocious). Specifically:

I. Perfect seeing, without a quiver.

II. Slight undulations, with moments of calm lasting several seconds.

III. Moderate seeing, larger air tremors.

IV. Poor seeing with constant troublesome undulations.

V. Very bad seeing, scarcely allowing the making of a rough sketch.

When you keep notes of your observations—as you should unless you are just sightseeing—that scale makes a handy shorthand to describe the atmospheric seeing conditions.

As you may have guessed, nights of perfect seeing are rare. The more the stars twinkle, the worse the seeing. All this has nothing to do with the *clarity* of the atmosphere. During a slight haze the air is often remarkably steady, very suitable for the observation of bright objects such as the planets.

Now let's take a quick tour through the sky to see what you can observe with a telescope.

Observing the Sun

I'll start the tour with the sun. To repeat a warning:

Never look at the sun through any telescope.

A brief exposure of an eye to the sun can cause serious, permanent eye damage. That danger exists even during an eclipse of the sun. And the warning certainly applies to the finder telescope also. It's wise to put *both* lens caps on the finder when observing in daylight. And don't leave your telescope unattended for a minute. Your child, or a neighbor's, may just take a notion to have a quick look.

There are several safe methods for observing the sun. Putting a dark filter somewhere near the eyepiece is not one of them. Gelatin filters can melt; even filters made for welders' goggles have cracked from the heat.

For a quick look at the sun, a white projection screen attached to the telescope is fine. Some manufacturers supply them with their telescopes. You can buy the whole assembly for others. Or construct one yourself from simple materials—lab clamps and an aluminum rod, for example.

You'll always have more light than you need. So it is a good idea to "stop down" the opening of your telescope to keep the optics cool. A cardboard with a hole in the center, mounted a few inches in front of your telescope—to permit air circulation—achieves that effect.

The sun's apparent diameter, like the moon's, is about $\frac{1}{2}$ degree. So you'll need a low-magnification eyepiece to project the image of the entire sun. The farther the projection screen is from the eyepiece, the larger the image will be, just as pulling the screen away from a film or slide projector increases image size. It will not compete with the 30-inch (76 cm)-diameter image of the sun at Kitt Peak observatory, where it is projected through a 500-foot (150 m) tunnel. But it will be large enough to see sunspots.

(Some sunspots can be seen with the naked eye. Proof: Chinese astronomers recorded them before the invention of the telescope. The technique is simple and safe: Observe when the sun has just risen or is about to set, *and* use a very dark filter.)

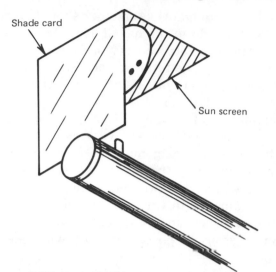

Shade card

Sun screen

Fig. 66. Projecting the image of the sun (briefly) on a white screen with a Newtonian reflector. For a refractor or other straight-through telescope the sun screen would be at right angles to the line of sight; a shade card with a small circle cut out would be between the eyepiece and the screen. READ WARNING in text.

To see the porridge-like *granulations* of the sun's surface, *faculae* (bright clouds floating above the surface), and *flares* (solar eruptions), you'll use higher magnification, projecting only part of the sun.

If you have more than a passing interest in solar phenomena, you may want to use a device that slips over the front end of your telescope. It works on the principle of the one-way window: The bootlegger could see you clearly, but you saw only yourself in a mirror. The mirrored surface reflects almost all of the sunlight, letting only $1/100$ of 1 percent enter the telescope.

If you become really serious about solar observation—by inclination or because you have to work nights—you can do systematic observations. Sunspots are ever changing in number, size, and location. It's fascinating to watch the progress of a group of spots from day to day. About thirteen days after the spots have disappeared from view, the

rotation of the sun will bring some of them back again on the other limb (edge).

Amateurs all over the world keep track of sunspots and supplement the data of the professional observatories, which have their overcast days. It requires no additional equipment beyond tracing paper, a pencil, and a grid, which you can draw yourself. These simple tools, with the aid of a conversion table, translate the apparent location of sunspots into solar latitude and longitude.

If you want to participate in this work, write to: Solar Group, American Association of Variable Star Observers, 187 Concord Avenue, Cambridge, Massachusetts 02138. A stamped self-addressed envelope will bring you all the information.

Observing the Moon

The moon undoubtedly has drawn more people to a telescope than any other object.

One of the earliest observers, Sir William Lower, as quoted by Patrick Moore, described the full moon as resembling a tart his cook had baked: "There some bright stuffe, there some dark, and so confusedlie all over."

From the chapter on binoculars you already know that the time of full moon is not best for seeing details on the moon. Whatever instrument you use, it'll be a vast improvement over the early 1600s instrument of Sir William.

The nightly, even hourly, changes near the edge of the lighted area—the terminator—are a fascinating spectacle.

Before long you may want to learn the names of each sea—about a dozen in all—and some prominent craters. Figure 61 will serve as a start. Some observers get as addicted to collecting lunar features as other people do to making lists of birds sighted or wildflowers identified. Other observers are content to watch a few examples of each of the major lunar features: mountain ranges, craters, crater chains, walled plains, ring plains, domes, and rilles. (*Rille* is a German word meaning "cleft" or "ravine.")

A single moon map, such as you'll find, for instance, in Norton's *Star Atlas,* or in most astronomy books in your public library, will get you nicely started. For more detailed views you may like the presentation in *A Field Guide to the Stars and Planets,* by Donald H. Menzel (Houghton Mifflin Co.). A dozen right-hand pages show superb photographs of sections of the moon; the facing left pages identify the features.

For even more serious observers there is, for example, *The Amateur Astronomer's Photographic Lunar Atlas,* by Henry H. Hatfield (Lutterworth Press, London). (For an American supplier, see advertisements in *Sky and Telescope.*)

All moon maps used to show the moon's South Pole on top, as you see it in a straight-through telescope, with the left margin (near the Mare Crisium) labeled west, the right margin (near Grimaldi) labeled east. But recently the International Astronomical Union decided to label the sides as an astronaut would see them and put north on top. That decision has proved unpopular with observers because it does not conform with what they see in a telescope. Many recent moon maps show the moon as before, only switching the *labels* east for west.

The moon, when seeing is good, can stand your maximum magnification. The brightness of the image, even at such magnification, may bother you. Remedy: An eyepiece filter. Some observers use a photographic filter, such as a dark red one, claiming it enhances contrast at the same time that it cuts down on brightness. But it colors everything a gory red. For that reason a neutral-density filter, which leaves colors unaltered, is the choice of many moon watchers.

The moon may not be as dead as one might believe. Occasional flashes of light have been reported. Are these meteors striking the moon's surface? Someone has calculated that a 10-pound (4½ kg) meteor should create a flash visible to the naked eye.

Then there are reports of *transient lunar phenomena*. The term was coined by Patrick Moore. If you think you may be interested in watching for TLPs—white clouds, pale luminous haze, and red events—read his *New Guide to the Moon* (W. W. Norton). The chances of catching any of these phenomena are small. Only the hardiest observers will stick with such a program, which is doubly frustrating for this reason: If you do happen to catch such an event, unless some other observer also reports it nobody will believe you.

If you want a program of serious work, you could try *lunar occultations*.

The most obvious motion of the moon and the stars is their apparent hourly westward drift caused by the rotation of Earth. But the moon also moves *eastward* among the stars, completing one circuit in a little less than a month, so the moon often passes between an observer on Earth and a star. That's called an occultation.

During an occultation a star suddenly disappears. This *immersion* is so abrupt because the moon lacks a twilight-causing atmosphere. An hour later at most, the star emerges, equally suddenly, on the other side of the moon.

The time of immersion and *emersion* is one of the best ways to check the exact period of rotation of Earth, which enters into all astronomical calculations.

Until recently it was assumed that our planet rotated at a constant rate. Any discrepancy between the observed position of the moon and its predicted position was blamed on some minor flaw in the equations used in the calculation.

Modern astronomical clocks keep time to such an accuracy—a tiny fraction of a second per year—that we now know the rate of rotation is not uniform. Between the beginning of this century and the time this is written in 1979 the errors have added up to a total of almost fifty seconds!

You can see that this is an important problem. To get exact corrections takes many observations.

The moon is so close to us that it may occult a star at your location yet pass clear of that star at the nearest observatory. Given your exact location, and the exact time of occultation of a given star, the astronomers at the Royal Greenwich Observatory—the world clearinghouse for these data—can calculate the total error on that date. By combining your observations with many others, they arrive at a figure accurate to one hundredth of one second.

Your observation needs to be timed only to the nearest half second. That requires only one piece of equipment: a radio that receives short wave. Station WWV in Boulder, CHU in Ottawa, and others continuously broadcast time signals on several frequencies. They announce the time in plain English, then give a beep or tick every second. You just count beeps from the last full minute, or start a stopwatch.

All the stars used in this work—some fifty in all—are brighter than magnitude 7.5, so no fancy telescope is needed. You always observe the star at the *un*lighted side of the moon, either immersing or emerging. You'll find it easier to time the disappearance.

The Observer's Handbook, published annually by the Royal Astronomical Society of Canada, a paperback of 120 pages, each year gives occultations for Halifax, Montreal, Toronto, Winnipeg, Edmonton, and Vancouver. It lets you calculate the corrected time if you live within 300 miles of one of these cities—in New England, or the state of Washington, for example.

A few of the stars used are double stars, and you may notice what looks like a gradual disappearance, or a pausing of the star when in contact with the moon.

To try your hand at this type of work, you can start without predictions. (*Sky and Telescope,* however, supplies some.) Just watch for a star to disappear or emerge. The next step would be to time that event, perhaps with a borrowed short-wave receiver (and stopwatch).

If, after a try, you think you might want to contribute to this program regularly, get in touch with the International Occultation Timing Association, current address 4032 North Ashland Avenue, Chicago, Illinois 60613. Members of the IOTA receive quarterly newsletters.

Occasionally the moon's upper or lower limb just barely obscures a star. Such a *grazing* occultation gives astronomers an accurate check on the declination of the moon, while a central occultation serves as a check on its right ascension.

Since the moon is not a smooth disk but presents a ragged outline, the star in a grazing occultation may disappear and reappear several times.

The track on which you'll be able to observe a graze is only a couple of miles wide. For a small fee, the IOTA will send you a computer printout of points along the limits of any particular graze, and instructions for setting up a field trip for best observation.

You may wonder how the time signals, say of WWV, are generated. Basically, by one of those superaccurate clocks. But when lunar occultations and other astronomical observations indicate the need, a *leap second* is added at the end of the months of December and/or June. That keeps the world's clocks in step with the variable speed of rotation of Earth.

Eclipses of the moon occur when the shadow of Earth falls on the moon. When only part of the moon gets into the shadow, you see a partial eclipse; when the entire moon enters the shadow, a total eclipse. Unlike total eclipses of the sun, which can be seen only in a narrow strip of Earth, a total eclipse of the moon can be seen wherever the moon at the time is above the horizon.

If you have a telescope, you'll hardly pass up an eclipse of the moon. The progress of the shadow across the features of the lunal landscape is well worth watching. Total eclipses of the moon also bring with them unpredictable changes in its color.

Observing the Planets

Most people's first view of the planets through a typical amateur telescope is a disappointment. They have seen photographs taken under ideal conditions through the world's largest telescopes. Worse, they may have seen artists' paintings based on such photographs.

How large an image can you expect? The largest will be that of Venus when nearest Earth. Its diameter then is 66 seconds of arc—about $1/28$ of the diameter of the moon. That's about the size of one of the larger moon craters. And that's for the most favorable planet at the most favorable time. Do I want to discourage you from watching the planets? Far from it. But be realistic in your expectations.

Mercury is a difficult planet to observe. You'll recall that only at a few periods each year does it get far enough from the sun to be seen with the naked eye, low in the sky before sunrise or after sunset. Low in the sky means rotten seeing through a telescope. So professional astronomers observe Mercury at the most favorable times in daylight, when it is high in the sky. They use the planet's predicted position and the setting circles on their telescopes.

Extreme caution is needed to avoid getting the sun in view. Also, you must shade the telescope from the sun or tube currents will become intolerable. A beach umbrella over the whole setup will do it.

Frankly, you won't see much. The disk, at best, is $1/5$ the size of the figure just given for Venus, $1/140$ the diameter of the moon. At

100× magnification you'll see the moonlike phases, but that's about all.

Professional astronomers had convinced themselves that Mercury always shows the same side to the sun, just as the moon does to Earth. On that basis they had produced maps of the visible features on Mercury.

Then, in the 1960s, radar revealed that Mercury rotates on its axis. So much for surface features seen through even professional telescopes. (Mercury's moonlike surface has since been mapped in great detail by the Mariner 10 spacecraft.)

In November 1986, 1993, and 1999 Mercury will pass in front of the disk of the sun, looking like a sharply defined single sunspot. *Sky and Telescope* will give exact dates and times. When the sun is below the horizon at the time of transit, you will, of course, not see it.

Venus, by comparison with Mercury, is an easy object to observe, available for months on end, higher in the sky, and easily found in daylight.

Its phases are easily seen. But the *ashen light,* the unlighted part of the disk that corresponds to the "old moon in the arms of the new," is only rarely seen.

The surface of Venus is forever hidden from view. What we see are the tops of ever-present, unbroken clouds.

Mars, by contrast, permits us to see the surface with only occasional dust storms obscuring the landscape.

The diameter of the disk of Mars—it always appears at least gibbous—varies from $3\frac{1}{2}$ to 25 seconds of arc. At opposition—that is, when we are between Mars and the sun—the disk appears largest and brightest.

Near opposition is the best time for observation. The greater the magnitude (given in the calendar), the more favorable the opposition. The one in February 1980 (magnitude -1.0) is poor compared to that of September 1988 (magnitude -2.5), for example.

With good seeing conditions, at favorable

oppositions, you will make out some surface markings and color shadings on Mars. They'll drift with the rotation of Mars (about one half hour longer than that of Earth).

You'll also see the white cap—carbon dioxide snow—over the pole where at that time it's winter on Mars.

Mars has two tiny, odd-shaped, moons, Phobos (FOH-bos) and Deimos (DAY-mohs). They are of magnitudes 11 and 12 but are totally overwhelmed by the light from Mars itself.

Jupiter always presents a virtually full appearance. At worst, its disk appears half as large again as Mars at its most favorable. At best, it is twice the largest diameter of Mars. What you'll see mainly are bands of clouds, parallel to Jupiter's equator.

The bands are the consequence of Jupiter's rapid rotation. More than eleven times the diameter of Earth, Jupiter manages to turn on its axis once in less than ten hours. That rotation is also responsible for the noticeable flattening of Jupiter.

The outstanding feature in even a small telescope is the famed Great Red Spot, probably discovered in 1664. It's almost four Earth diameters wide, one Earth diameter high. It has paled and darkened since its discovery and shifts somewhat in position. The best current explanation: It is the top of a stationary hurricane, the red coloring being caused by gases brought from lower regions to cloud top level.

Of the baker's dozen of Jupiter's moons, four are easily seen. In fact, they were discovered by Galileo with his primitive telescope. These Galilean moons named—outward—Io, Europa, Ganymede, and Callisto, or simply I, II, III, and IV, all vary in magnitude around mean magnitudes between 5 and 6.

All four are in the equatorial plane of Jupiter; their periods of revolution range from about 1.8 to 17 days. So there is plenty of action to observe: eclipses, when a moon enters Jupiter's shadow; immersions and emersions, when it disappears or reappears behind Jupiter; transits, when a moon—much darker than the planet itself—passes between us and Jupiter; and shadows cast by the moons on the clouds of Jupiter.

Historically, these events gave the first measurement of the speed of light. Before the use of chronometers and radio time signals, they were a means of getting accurate time, a necessity for getting one's position at sea.

Saturn, because of its system of rings, is the most spectacular of the planets. With the rings included, the image of Saturn at its most favorable is only a little smaller across than the diameter of Jupiter. The disk of Saturn resembles Jupiter's, without the red spot and with much less detail in the cloud bands.

The outside diameter of the ring system is more than twice the diameter of the disk itself. Seen from Earth, the rings form concentric ellipses around the planet's equator. Because of the inclination of Saturn's axis to its orbit, we see the rings from above for about half the time it takes the planet to circle the sun ($29\frac{1}{2}$ years), and from below for the other half. In between, the rings disappear (e.g., in 1980 and 1995). They are then edge on, or else only their edges are illuminated by the sun. The edge is so thin—a few miles at most—that the effect seen from Earth is the same.

The rings are not solid, but made of loose pieces—estimates vary from gravel, to brick, to small boulder size—that circle Saturn independently. Proof: An eighth-magnitude or brighter star occulted by the ring remains visible.

The rings, A and B, labeled from the outside toward the planet, are easily seen. The debris-free area between them, the Cassini division, is at times more difficult to make out. The next ring, going inward, the C or crepe ring, requires good atmospheric seeing

Fig. 67. The rings of Saturn.

and superb optics. A much fainter ring, D, almost touching the planet, was discovered only in 1969. That gives an indication of the difficulty in seeing it.

Saturn casts its shadow on the rings when the sun is to one side of our line of sight.

Saturn has at least ten moons, most of them in the plane of the rings but outside of the ring system. Four or five of them and the shadows they cast on Saturn are visible through a 6-inch telescope.

Uranus, when nearest to us, should, according to some authorities, be just visible to the naked eye. But its discovery as a planet took some 170 years of telescope use. (It had been mapped as a fixed star for more than 100 years before that.)

It takes 50× magnification to see Uranus as a greenish blue disk. And that's all you'll see at any magnification. Don't blame your telescope or the atmosphere: Photographs taken through telescopes lifted into the stratosphere failed to record any detail.

Neptune is scarcely visible, no more than a small greenish disk, through the largest telescopes. You'll be lucky if you can see it even as a disk.

Pluto needs an 8-inch-aperture telescope to show it at all. Then it'll look like a fixed star without any indication of a disk.

If you have the right equipment, experience, and infinite patience, you may engage in a systematic program of observing planets. Your nearest astronomy club may have a program going or put you in touch

with a club that has. The Association of Lunar and Planetary Observers, at this time, does not seem interested. It did not answer requests for information sent with stamped self-addressed envelope.

Comets

Spectacular comets are rare. In the last century, there were three; in this century, none since 1910. There have been a few comets that you could see with the naked eye if you knew where to look, usually low in the east before sunrise or low in the west after sunset.

With a telescope you may see, on average, six to eight comets a year. More than half of them are periodic returners, whose position in the sky is predicted months in advance in astronomy magazines. Perhaps two or three "new" comets are discovered in an average year. "New" here means that their orbits had not been calculated before.

At discovery, or rediscovery, a comet is typically at the distance of Mars from the sun, a fuzzy object of total magnitude between 8 and 10. That's well within the range of even a modest telescope.

The comet then brightens and normally grows a tenuous tail as it approaches the sun. For a short period it disappears in the twilight, only to come out on the opposite side of the sun: in the evening sky if before it was in the morning sky.

If the comet happens to be visible to the naked eye, finding it in the telescope is no problem. Just use a low-magnification eyepiece, or your finder, to get a large field.

If you have advance notice of a comet's position, plot it in your star atlas. If the predictions are for dates five days apart, plot the two points and search near the line connecting them. Setting circles—RA and DEC dials—help, but constellations and bright stars in them are usually enough to start your search.

What are the chances of your discovering a comet and having it named after you? Not good. In a recent period, 57 percent of comet discoveries were by-products of some other astronomical program, such as routine sky photography to find stars that suddenly flared up. Many of the remaining 43 percent were found at professional observatories searching for comets.

At the Skalnate Pleso observatory in Czechoslovakia, nineteen were found in eleven years. One astronomer there, Antonin Mrkos, alone discovered eleven in one year.

But in comet hunting, professionals have no great advantage over amateurs, except that they get paid for their time. The equipment needed is simple: a rich-field telescope of at least 4-inch (100 mm) aperture. "Rich-field" means "wide-field," what a photographer would call wide-angle. To make the search efficient, the field should be 1 to 3 degrees at magnifications of 25× to 40×.

Some comet hunters have used refractors, others even monster binoculars. It would seem a 6-inch Newtonian of 30-inch focal length would be a good choice. Until you know that that's what you want to go in for, your more common 48-inch reflector will do nicely.

Comets can approach the sun from any direction, but statistics show your best chance of discovering a comet is to sweep the eastern sky before sunrise.

Many mornings will be spoiled by clouds, rain, perhaps fog. The moon—in the waning gibbous phase—will eliminate other mornings by washing out dim objects. Close to the horizon, you'll run into the atmospheric extinction effect. And at the first sign of dawn, you may as well go back to bed.

But suppose you have a perfect morning. Proceed with overlapping sweeps. For that a simple altazimuth mount is handier than an equatorial mount. It lets you sweep horizontally, then raise (or lower) the scope about half a field height, and sweep back. Raise (or lower) again by the same amount, and sweep again. . . .

Your eyes will have to be dark-adapted, and you should use averted vision whenever you can.

Eventually you'll find a fuzzy dim spot. Is it a comet? First use a higher magnification that may resolve the hazy patch into several stars. If that test is negative, the spot could be a nebula or a galaxy. To eliminate them, look first in your star atlas. If it's a bright one, as such objects go, it will be indicated there. If it isn't, consult Dreyer's *New General Catalogue* (reprint 1953, Royal Astronomical Society, London), which lists seven thousand such objects.

By the time you have looked there, a comet would have moved a tiny bit against the background of stars. If it's still dark, check that. A nebula or galaxy stays put.

If dawn arrived in the meantime, you'll have to wait until tomorrow.

If the object moved, send a telegram to Harvard Observatory, Oak Ridge, Massachusetts, giving date, hour, and minute of discovery, the object's position as accurately as possible—from the nearest star in the atlas—and an estimate of its extension—from the field diameter of your eyepiece—and magnitude. Maybe it *is* a new comet, and just maybe no one else has reported it yet.

One amateur is said to have discovered a comet when he tried out a new eyepiece. A Japanese comet hunter, Kaoru Ikeya, found his first comet after 109 nights. Alcock, a British amateur, in fourteen hundred hours of sweeping over a period of twelve years discovered four comets.

15

Observing with a Telescope:
The Galaxy and Beyond

Double Stars

Two stars seen with the naked eye may just seem accidentally close together. The classic example is Mizar (MEYE-zuhr), the second star from the outboard end of the handle of the Big Dipper. Its dimmer neighbor, Alcor (AL-kor), has been used as a test for good vision since antiquity.

True double stars, or binary stars, form a gravitational system in which each star revolves around the center of gravity of the pair. In a telescope, Mizar breaks up into such a pair. Its companion—Comes (KOH-meez) is the technical term for that—is of fourth magnitude.

About one star in four or five has a companion; some have several. Some double stars can be separated only in large telescopes; some betray their presence only in the spectroscope.

But there are thousands of binaries acces-sible to modest telescopes. Many are mapped and listed in Norton's. Since the individual stars move, they change their posi-tion relative to one another (position angle) and their separation.

The separation is given in seconds of arc: e.g., 14″ for Mizar. The eye can just resolve 4′ of arc (240″); 8′ (480″) makes for easier seeing. To get the magnification needed for *just* splitting a pair, divide 240 by the separa-tion of the pair. To get the magnification needed for *easy* splitting, divide 480 by their separation.

> EXAMPLE: 480 ÷ 14 is about 35. An eyepiece that gives 35× magnification will easily split the Mizar double. The same eyepiece might just reveal two stars only 7″ apart.

There is one more thing to be considered. The resolution limit of your telescope, dis-cussed earlier, sets the final limit.

A dim star close to a bright one is much

more difficult to separate—for example, the ninth-magnitude companion of Sirius. And when the atmosphere is in turmoil, you'll never be sure whether you saw one star or two.

These very difficulties get some observers hooked on this type of observation. Others go on to other sights after splitting the double double of Epsilon Lyrae, a little west and north of Vega.

Clusters, Nebulae, and Galaxies

Sightseeing in the sky by simply aiming the telescope at any part of the Milky Way is great. Some areas of the Milky Way are richer, others poorer, in stars, but for the gourmet there is endless pleasure in just scanning the sky. Also, on nights of poor seeing the part of the Milky Way nearest your zenith will give pleasure, while the planets are just about hopeless.

There are other objects for sightseeing: the clusters, nebulae, and galaxies at the limit of naked-eye visibility, about which you read in Chapter 10, on binoculars.

You may want to scan the night sky and find more of these objects on your own. With a star atlas and setting circles, you can then identify the objects you see.

Even without setting circles, you can do that by using the diameter of the field in the eyepiece you are using, or in your finder, for a scale.

You could go the opposite route: finding nebulae and clusters marked in your atlas. Many observers have had uncounted hours of pleasure at their telescopes—and learned a lot in the process—by finding *Messier* objects.

Charles Messier is credited with having discovered at least thirteen comets. He became interested in searching for comets in 1758, the year in which Halley predicted the comet of 1682 would return. (Edmund Halley, British astronomer royal, was the first astronomer to calculate the orbit of a comet. This comet's returns have now been documented as far back as the third century B.C. Halley did not see the return he predicted. He had died in 1742.)

Messier searched for what we now call Halley's comet—most recent return 1910, expected again in 1986—but an amateur astronomer in Dresden spotted it first.

Some authors think Messier's list of nebulous objects was simply a by-product of his searching for comets. I have another theory: Messier, like anyone searching for comets, was frequently fooled by non-comet look-alikes. He mapped these objects so he would not be fooled again. Later he published his list in three installments, spread over thirteen years. In all he listed 103 objects; 6 more were added two years later by one of his colleagues.

Three objects on Messier's list don't belong on it. M40 is a double star. Either Messier or the typesetter goofed on M102; it is a repetition of the preceding entry, M101. M91 is a mystery according to reference books I've consulted. Could it have been an honest comet, which, at the time Messier logged it, moved so slowly that he mistook it for one of those pesky fakes?

Most of the remaining 106 Messier objects can be seen through a 3-inch refractor. Many serious owners of 6-inch reflectors have succeeded in finding every one of the Messier objects. And you don't have to travel to the Southern Hemisphere; Messier's catalog was compiled in Paris (latitude 49°N).

You get the list and a finder map of Messier objects as an insert in Norton's *Star Atlas*. It is also reprinted in many other books, including the *Canadian Observer's Handbook*. There you'll also find shorthand descriptions of the type of each of these diffuse objects. "Nebula," in Messier's time, included many hazy objects. Now, strictly speaking, we distinguish between a nebula—part of our own galaxy—and an external galaxy, which may be elliptical, spiral, or irregular.

Collecting Messier objects will keep you busy for many hours. In your searches you will "discover" many more interesting objects. But they will already be listed in the NGC (*New General Catalogue*) or some more recent publication. The probability of your finding a diffuse object that has escaped the cameras of the great observatories is nil.

Variable Stars

Some stars change in apparent brightness—magnitude.

Astronomers have found that stars, according to their mass, go through typical life cycles in which they change size, color, and magnitude. These changes, however, take millions of years. The changes in magnitude I am talking about here are a matter of days, or at most years.

There is some slight evidence that one such variable star had been noticed for a long time. Its name, Algol, translates into "ghost" or "demon" (it has the same root as "ghoul"), perhaps because of its ghostly behavior.

It's easy enough to observe without any optical aid. For finding it, use Figure 41.

Algol is normally of magnitude 2.2, not much dimmer than nearby Mirfak, and about as bright as Polaris. But within a few hours it drops to magnitude 3.5. Within a few hours it recovers its normal brightness. That process repeats at intervals of 2 days 20 hours 49 minutes. (You can find the dates and times of minima for the current month in *Sky and Telescope*.)

What we are watching is Algol being partially eclipsed by a dimmer companion. About one out of every five variable stars is explained by binary star mechanics.

Some of these mechanics are more complicated than Algol's—for example, a system of two stars too close to be resolved through telescopes. Both contribute to the overall brightness, so you'll get very different magnitude measurements depending on which star eclipses the other.

A few binary stars are so close together that the gravitational attraction of one distorts the shape of the other. You'll then get very complicated changes in magnitude depending on whether you are looking at the bulges sideways or from the back.

A few variable binaries are so close together that luminous material is actually exchanged between them.

Naked-eye astronomers could easily have discovered the strange behavior of Algol, but it was not described in the West until 1782. The first variable star discovered was *not* an eclipsing star. In 1596 David Fabricius, a Dutch observer, found that Cetus (SEE-tuhs), the Whale, contained a new second-magnitude star. He followed it until it sank below naked-eye visibility. (Such decline is to be expected from a new star.) But then he found a bright star in the same place again in 1609.

Johann Bayer, in his famous *Uranometria*, published in 1603, had designated a star in that position as Omicron Ceti. Bayer assigned Greek letters to stars in each constellation in order of brightness. Since omicron is the fifteenth letter of the Greek alphabet, and the brightest star in Cetus is of second magnitude, there was something obviously strange here.

It took another thirty years to establish that these sightings were of the same star, which faded and brightened. It was given the name Mira (MEYE-ruh), "miraculous one." Another thirty years later, it was finally established that the period of this strange behavior is about eleven months.

The first edition of the Encyclopaedia Britannica (1771) gives several explanations for the variation in magnitude of "periodic" stars. One: The stars are covered with large clusters of dark spots and rotate slowly, "by which means they must disappear when the side covered with spots is turned toward us.'' Two: According to Pierre Maupertius (1698–1759) ''some stars by their prodigious quick rotation on their axes, may not only assume the figures of oblate spheroids (as do Earth, Jupiter, etc.) but that by the great centrifugal force arising from such rotations they may become the figures of millstones, or be reduced to flat circular planes, so thin as to be quite invisible when their edges are turned toward us, as Saturn's ring is in such position.''

We now know, without question, the true cause, which seems much more unlikely than the explanations given: These stars pulsate, swelling and shrinking.

Four out of every five variable stars fall into this class. Some, like Mira, have periods between 150 and 500 days. Many more have periods of only a few days. Yet others, like Betelgeuse, are unpredictable, hence are classed as semiregular or irregular.

You can contribute to fundamental astronomical knowledge by systematically observing variable stars in a worldwide program. A few hours a week at your telescope and some paperwork once a month are all that's required.

The coordinating organization, the American Association of Variable Star Observers (AAVSO), 187 Concord Avenue, Cambridge, Massachusetts 02138, actively looks for new observers. Anyone above age sixteen can become a full member. (But they will get you started and sell you materials at members' prices at any age.) A few members have sent in monthly reports for sixty consecutive years!

A stamped, self-addressed envelope to the above address will get you not only information, but instructions, a finder chart, and a practice chart. The technique, basically, is to compare visually the variable star with several nearby nonvariable stars for which the magnitude is printed on the practice chart.

It sounds almost impossible, but with this method you'll probably get within 0.2 magnitudes on the first try, and advance to an accuracy of 0.1 magnitudes after some nights' practice.

The equipment needed ranges from binoculars, through small portable telescopes, to near-professional-size instruments. There is ample work for all. In 1844, when cooperative observation of variable stars started, only 18 stars were known to be variable. Now 20,000 stars are so listed in star catalogs. The AAVSO program covers about 1,000 stars with close to 200,000 observations a year.

Professional astronomers routinely use data supplied by AAVSO. Occasionally they request special observations. Example: A spacecraft measures soft X-ray radiation from certain stars. To tie in these observations with the emission of visible light, they need simultaneous measurements from the ground. AAVSO in such cases mails out ''Alerts'' asking members to make the requested observations.

Variable star observations have enormously advanced our astronomical knowledge.

You may have wondered how astronomers have measured the distances of stars and galaxies printed in astronomy books.

Measuring the diameter of a star is out of the question. That system already reaches its limits for Neptune and Pluto. (Occultations of stars by these planets give much better results.)

For nearby stars, astronomers use a method not unlike that of a land surveyor: They measure the change in angle when they move their instrument. A surveyor may move his instrument a few hundred yards (or meters). Moving a telescope from one end of a continent to the other, however (or even observing at the same time from Hawaii and Greenwich, half a world apart), gives no measurable angular difference.

But there is another way of moving an astronomical telescope: Do nothing at all, just let Earth's motion around the sun shift your position. The mean distance from Earth to sun, the Astronomical Unit, is about 93 million miles (150 million km). Moving your observing station that far might give a measurable angle.

A star a certain distance away should show a displacement—*parallax* is the technical term—of 1 second of arc. That provides an astronomical distance unit: Such a star would be at a distance of 1 *parsec*.

Knowing the speed of light (186,000 miles or 300,000 km per second), you could easily calculate that the light from a star at that distance would take 3.26 years to reach us. The star 1 parsec distant could just as well be said to be 3.26 light-years away.

One second of arc—$^1/_{3600}$ part of a degree—is a very small angle. It's about the angle a dime—or any coin about 18 mm in diameter—presents when it's 2.3 miles (3.7 km) distant.

Actually, there is no star close enough to give a 1-second parallax. The nearest one, part of the multiple star system of Alpha Centauri, which you know as Rigil Kent, gives a parallax of only ¾ of 1 second of arc, corresponding to a distance of 4.3 light-years.

Fewer than fifty stars show a parallax of even 0.2 parsec (16 light-years). So how do astronomers estimate the distance of stars and galaxies millions of light-years away? Answer: from observation of the period of certain variable stars.

In 1914 Henrietta Leavitt of the Harvard Observatory studied variable stars in the Large Magellanic Cloud. She concentrated on short-period variables, specifically Cepheid variables, named after the prototype in Cepheus (SEE-fee-uhs) with periods of 2 to 40 days. She made a fundamental discovery: the brighter a Cepheid, the longer its period.

This period-luminosity relationship suddenly provided astronomers with a yardstick to the visible universe.

We have known for a long time how light diminishes with distance. (Move a candle twice as far from you and you'll get one quarter the amount of light.) That easily translates into stellar magnitudes.

Now measure the magnitude of some Cepheids in another galaxy, and determine their periods. Simple arithmetic then lets you calculate how much farther that galaxy is from us than the Large Magellanic Cloud. (Assuming the Large Magellanic Cloud to be 160,000 light-years from us, you'd get 2.1 million l.y. for the Andromeda Galaxy (M31); M49 and M104, two galaxies in Virgo, give 37 million l.y.

In 1929 Edwin Hubble, measuring the displacement of spectral lines toward the red, discovered that galaxies were speeding away from us, the faster the farther they were from Earth.

The distance of the galaxies he investigated had been determined from Cepheids they contained. So the discovery of the concept of the expanding universe owes its discovery to careful observations of variable stars.

16

Astrophotography with a Telescope

Photography of celestial objects lets you share your observations with other observers. It also lets you show what fascinates you to people who consider your time spent at the telescope a form of mild insanity.

Photography is not only a means of recording what you see through the telescope. The negative records *more* than the eye can see.

How can that be? If you look at a spot in the sky where you can't see any stars even with totally dark-adapted eyes, looking longer will not show any stars there. Now take a photograph of that bare patch. A short exposure will not show any stars there either. But double the exposure time and you will see some stars in the bare patch; quadruple it and it'll show many more.

Photography of celestial objects presents many technical challenges. Mastering just one specialty—star fields, the moon, the planets, or deep-sky objects (outside our own galaxy)—may keep you busy for months. Mastering them all will keep your interest for years.

Don't expect your first efforts to compete with Mount Palomar photographs. Don't even expect them to compare with the "amateur" photographs published in astronomical magazines. These photographs are the pick of the crop, often taken with very sophisticated equipment, by people who may have worked in one specialty for years.

Also there is the secret of a spectacular garden: Weed out the things that aren't doing well.

At a recent symposium I admired a board of mounted sky photographs and the slides presented by one of the speakers. When I congratulated him, he let me in on his secret: "My collection has less than fifty pictures. That's fifty out of five thousand exposures."

Obviously it'd be a good idea to cut your teeth on some easier subjects before tackling more difficult ones.

Camera Mounted on Telescope

Constellations and sections of the Milky Way are the easiest subjects. Let's look at them first. Most of the basic principles that apply here apply to other subjects of astrophotography.

With just a camera and a tripod, you can photograph star trails. You can already guess what it takes to picture the stars as little dots instead of streaks: an equatorial mount with clock drive.

You could buy a light telescope mount and mount your camera on it instead of a telescope. Or you could build one from readily available parts.

But you'll run into two snags. First, without a telescope it is not easy to set the polar axis of a portable mount accurately enough. So during a long time exposure your camera will not track the stars, even with the most accurate drive. Second, motor drives are not that accurate. Your camera will need some additional "guiding." For that, and all other types of astrophotography, you'll need a telescope.

The easiest solution is to mount your camera piggyback on your telescope, which is equatorially mounted and clock-driven. Many telescope makers supply a camera mount as an inexpensive accessory. You can also build one yourself, using perhaps a flash attachment bracket.

You can use almost any camera with a quality lens that allows time (or bulb) exposures. For all other astrophotography, the 35mm single-lens reflex camera with removable lens is first choice. But here you can use a camera with ground-glass focusing, $2\frac{1}{4}\times2\frac{1}{4}''$ (6×6cm) or $3\frac{1}{4}\times4\frac{1}{4}''$ (9×12cm) or larger.

The camera needs no shutter; you can control the exposure with a piece of

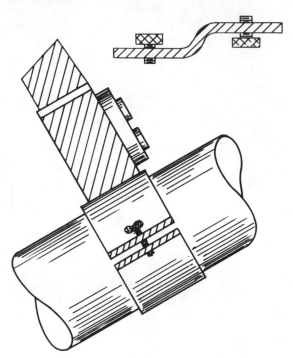

Fig. 68. Camera mounted on telescope. Insert: A simple camera bracket; left screw threads into telescope, right screw into camera.

cardboard after removing the lens cap. The cardboard is also useful for interrupting the exposure when a plane strays across the field of view of the camera.

The "speed" of the lens—the f/number when the diaphragm is wide open—does not matter for star photography. What matters is only the physical diameter of the lens. An f/2 50 mm lens has a clear aperture of about 25 mm (50 mm ÷ 2). An f/5.6 135 mm has almost the same aperture. For photographing the stars, the two are of the same speed. If on a given film one records stars down to magnitude 8.0 in a ten-minute exposure, so will the other.

That is contrary to all you have learned in everyday photography, which deals not with *points* of light but with extended lighted surfaces. Other objects of astrophotography—the moon, nebulae, planets, and comets—are such extended objects, for which the everyday rule applies. The *f*/5.6 lens requires about eight times the exposure of the *f*/2 lens.

Other rules of photography are not suspended. The longer-focus lens on the same film will show a smaller area of the sky. A lens of 2-inch diameter will take only one quarter the exposure time to produce the same images as a 1-inch lens.

That is the reason why some serious star-field photographers build their own cameras from such optics as World War II Aero Ektars of nearly 3-inch clear diameter, which take only one eighth the exposure time of a 1-inch lens.

On longer exposures any lens will record fainter stars than on shorter exposures. As a rule of thumb, you have to triple the exposure time to gain one magnitude.

But there is a limit. Eventually sky light will fog the background until it swallows the faintest star images. A sky that looks dark to us is not without light even in the dark of the moon and away from city lights. For a 1-inch diameter lens, that may limit you to stars of the eleventh magnitude; for a 2-inch diameter lens, to thirteenth magnitude.

In wide-field photography you have a good choice of film sizes. If you plan to show the result of your efforts as slides, you'll use 35mm film. If you want prints, you may prefer a larger film size where the negative is already bigger than the usual 3× enlargement of the smaller format. The best negatives (or transparencies) can be enlarged, of course.

You can use color or black and white film, process it yourself, or send your work out. Processing film yourself has many advantages. You can develop test shots and see the result in time to make the final exposure the same night. You can "push" development to get more speed out of a given film. And you can use high-contrast films, or films specially made for astrophotography, and special developers.

Developing black and white films isn't difficult. (I developed my first negatives on my eighth birthday.) Making same-size prints is just as easy. The equipment for either process is minimal, and the kitchen (or bathroom) sink serves as your darkroom.

If you send your work out, stick to common films. Also make sure the lab won't cut through your prize shots. Specify, for example, "uncut and unmounted" for 35mm slides.

You may think using the fastest films would let you overcome some of the difficulties of astrophotography. But there's a surprise: something with the forbidding name *reciprocity failure*. In simplest terms, a film that's fast—high ASA or DIN number—in sunlight or lighted rooms may become a slow film when used to photograph faint astronomical objects.

In usual photography you may expose a film at $\frac{1}{1000}$ second on some outdoor sport, but $\frac{1}{30}$ second for grandmother indoors, where the light is only about $\frac{1}{30}$ as bright according to your exposure meter. Both negatives will be properly exposed.

Or you may shoot something at $\frac{1}{1000}$ with the lens set to *f*/4. Now stop down to *f*/22, which admits only $\frac{1}{32}$ of the former amount of light. Set the shutter at $\frac{1}{30}$, and the two exposures will give identical results. That's reciprocity: less light—more time. Your exposure meter or automatic camera is based on it.

To visualize how reciprocity can fail in astrophotography, imagine yourself filling a five-gallon bucket that leaks a bit. If you fill it at the rate of five gallons per minute, it'll take about a minute to fill. At the rate of one gallon per minute, you'll take about five minutes to fill it. Reciprocity seems to be operating.

Now put the bucket under a spigot that's just dribbling a little to simulate the very small amount of light reaching the film from space. The bucket will never fill. The dimmest objects will never be recorded, however long you expose the film.

Exposure times for star fields will typically run from five minutes to one hour. During that time, to keep star images round rather than letting them become peanut-shaped, you'll have to correct for the accumulating errors of setting up your telescope and your drive speed. That's called guiding.

An illuminated reticle eyepiece—a set of cross hairs lit by a tiny bulb—lets you keep the telescope continuously aimed at a star. This trick may help you: Throw the image slightly out of focus until the star image just fills the central square between the cross hairs.

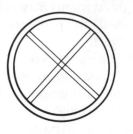

Fig. 69. Reticle (cross of fine wires).

You can practice tracking without film or camera. Set up the telescope as accurately as you can. Aim at any star in the area you plan to photograph.

Now move the telescope manually in right ascension. Turn the eyepiece until the star stays between the lines while you do that. If the star later moves up or down during guiding, you'll correct with the declination slow motion. If the star drifts *along* these lines away from the center square, you'll correct with the right ascension slow motion.

At first you'll tend to overcorrect, just as a learner oversteers an automobile or boat. But stick with it through some practice runs. Also, piggyback camera photography is very forgiving. Guiding errors that seem enormous in the eyepiece won't show on your developed and even enlarged photograph.

When you use the telescope not just as a guide (see below) you'll have to guide much more closely. Also, you won't be able to use the simple reticle. (The usual short, low-magnification finder telescope is no help either.) Then you'll use an *off-axis guider*. In that device, a tiny prism throws a small amount of light from the photographic field into a separate eyepiece (with lighted cross hairs). There you see your guiding errors enlarged. You can, of course, also use this attachment for piggyback photography.

If you find that you can't correct gently enough, perhaps some geared-down control knob is available for your particular drive. Even better for the right ascension drive is an electronic drive corrector that speeds up or slows down your drive motor.

As in most astrophotography, you usually have to find your exposure time by test. Take, for instance, exposures of 5, 10, 20, and 40 minutes and keep notes.

Primary-focus Photography

While reading about piggyback photography it may have occurred to you that you already have a large-diameter optical system—your telescope. If you have, say, a

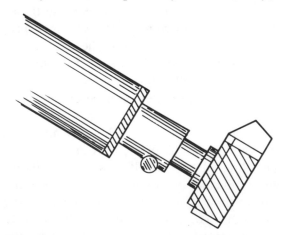

Fig. 70. Camera (without lens) mounted on telescope (without eyepiece) for primary-focus photography.

3-inch refractor, why not just use the telescope as an interchangeable lens on your 35mm single-lens reflex camera?

That's a good system, say, for photographing bright nebulae. You'll need, besides the off-axis guider, some adapter to fit the lens mount of your camera. A counterweight to balance the addition of camera and accessories to your telescope may also be needed.)

That same system also works well on commercial catadioptric telescopes, with the manufacturer providing the necessary hardware.

This setup (camera without lens, telescope without eyepiece) is known as primary-focus photography. Owners of Cassegrain telescopes often refer to it as "Cass focus" photography.

It does not work well on stock Newtonian telescopes. The primary focus—the focus of the main mirror—is somewhere inside the eyepiece mount. If you build a Newtonian reflector yourself, you can place the diagonal mirror closer to the primary mirror, and use the next larger size of diagonal mirror to get all of the image where the film in your camera will be. (A short extension tube will get the eyepiece at the proper distance for visual observation.)

As in everyday photography, the *f*/value of your optical system lets you calculate the exposure for any extended astronomical object—moon, nebulae, planets, comets—once you have found by test the correct exposure time for that object with that film but any other *f*/value.

You don't even have to make the test yourself. If you are using the same film as the photographer of a published photograph of the same object, you have a good starting point.

When comparing *f*/values, remember that doubling the *f*/number, as in all photography, requires *four* times the exposure to get the same result. In general: Divide the greater

Photo 14. Adjustable camera holder. Photo: Edmund Scientific Co.

f/number by the smaller one and multiply the result by itself.

> EXAMPLE: The caption of a photograph states that it was taken on a certain film when Jupiter was in opposition at *f*/15, at ¹/₁₀ of a second. Your setup gives *f*/45; you use the same film. How long should you expose?
> Answer: 45 ÷ 15 = 3; 3 × 3 = 9; 9 × ¹/₁₀ = 0.9. Expose for 1 second.

(Photographers will not often come across *f*/15; they use the markings on their lenses, say, *f*/11 or *f*/16. Telescopes are not cameras, and you'll work all the time with *f*/values not found on cameras.)

(On modern cameras you will not find a shutter speed of $^1/_{10}$ second, but many astrophotographers use shutters with speeds such as $^1/_5$, $^1/_{10}$, $^1/_{25}$, and you will find them under published photographs. When by calculation you get a shutter speed not available on your camera—as you almost always will—set your camera to the nearest speed. Better yet, bracket your exposure: Make one at the next faster, one at the next slower speed.)

Such calculations may save you much experimentation and film. Therefore I'll give you an approximate formula that lets you calculate the f/number for any astronomical setup.

In the primary-focus setup, the f/value is simply the f/value of your telescope. That, in turn, is its focal length divided by the diameter of its mirror, objective, or corrector.

Typically it will be f/15 for a refractor, f/10 to f/15 for a cadioptric instrument, and f/8 for a Newtonian telescope.

The size of the image in primary-focus photography will be modest. You can calculate the diameter of the image of the moon, with any photographic setup, in inches or millimeters, by a simple formula: Divide the focal length by 115. If you use inches, the result will be in inches; if you use millimeters, the result will be in millimeters.

A typical 3-inch refractor, a 5-inch Schmidt-Cassegrain, and a 6-inch Newtonian all have a focal length of 45 to 50 inches. In any of these the primary-focus image of the moon will then be about $^4/_{10}$ inch (10 mm) in diameter. (That makes this a poor setup for the moon.)

With any telescope, primary focus gives the lowest f/number, which means the shortest exposure. That makes it a good setup for a large, faint nebula or comet.

By the way, in photographing a comet, by whatever method, guide on the comet rather than the stars; let them become streaks.

The Afocal System

You may be tempted, before getting deeply into astrophotography, to simply attach your camera where normally your eye would be. If you have a single-lens reflex camera, even if the lens is not removable, you can try that.

The system is similar to the one described under photography through binoculars and works with any type of telescope.

The camera, focused for infinity, is somehow clamped to the telescope behind the eyepiece, which is focused in the usual way: that is, also for infinity. That may explain the name of the system: afocal (unfocused).

The distance between eyepiece and camera lens is critical, hence the need for reflex (or ground-glass) focusing. Use a magnifier.

Alignment of the film plane at right angles to the optical axis of the telescope is also critical. You will find that many eyepieces will not fill your 35mm format but light up

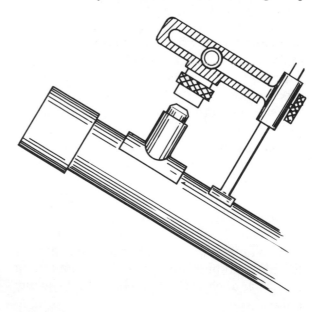

Fig. 71. Camera—its lens focused for infinity—mounted on telescope for afocal photography.

only a circle in the center. That's called vignetting.

Guiding is impossible. So you may want to use that system—except for experimentation—for the bright moon, which permits very short exposures.

To the primary-focus setup you now have added an eyepiece and the camera lens. Obviously, that will change the *f*/value of your system. To calculate it, do this: Multiply the *f*/number of your telescope by the focal length of your camera lens (in inches or millimeters) and divide by the focal length of your eyepiece (in the same units).

> EXAMPLE: Your *f*/8 reflector with a 2-inch (50 mm) camera lens and a ½-inch (12.5 mm) eyepiece becomes an *f*/32 system. (8 × 2 ÷ ½ = 32 or 8 × 50 ÷ 12.5 = 32.)

The focal length of your system, now known as the *equivalent focal length,* or *effective focal length* (EFL), has increased in the same ratio. Once you know the *f*/number of your system, you can find the EFL easily. Just multiply it by the diameter of the objective lens or mirror.

> EXAMPLE: The *f*/32 setup of the reflector in the last example has a 6-inch mirror. (32 × 6 = 192.) The EFL of your system is now 192 inches.

The magnification has, of course, also increased. The moon, by the formula given above, is now 192 ÷ 115, or about 1.7 inches (42 mm) in diameter, larger than your 35mm film.

Eyepiece Projection

You have already encountered eyepiece projection: We projected the image of the sun, suitably reduced in brightness, onto a white card. Here we project the image of other astronomical objects directly on the

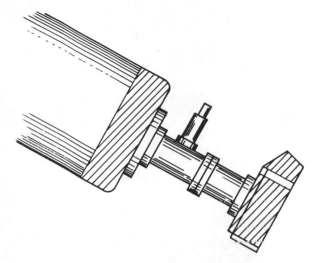

Fig. 72. Camera (without lens) coupled with off-axis guider and extension tubes to the telescope for eyepiece projection photography.

film in a camera from which the lens has been removed.

The setup is simple and keeps everything square: A tube that fits over your eyepiece at one end is screwed into your camera, where the lens was, at the other end. The eyepiece is racked out a bit farther than for visual observation. You check the focus on the screen of your reflex camera with a magnifier.

As in any projection system, the greater the distance from the lens—here, the eyepiece—the greater the magnification. To give you varying magnifications with the same telescope and eyepiece, the manufacturer provides either sliding tubes or a set of extension tubes, one screwing into the next.

The off-axis guider itself provides part of the tube assembly. You may have to attach a counterweight to the front of your telescope to rebalance the camera and tube assembly.

Eyepiece projection is the method of choice for much serious astrophotography. Orthoscopic or other well-corrected eyepiece designs give the best results.

The *f*/number of your system is the

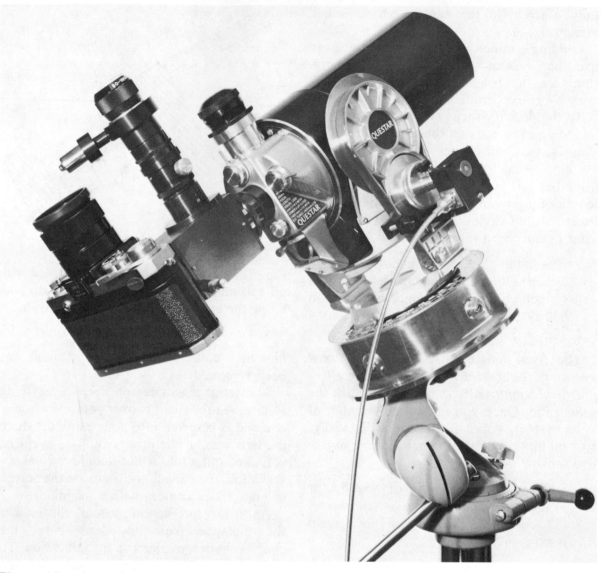

Photo 15. Astrophotography with off-axis guider (between eyepiece and camera), and **extra-fine adjuster on declination axis. Photo: Questar Corp.**

f/number of your telescope times the magnification of your projection system. For an *f*/8 telescope with 8× magnification you'll get *f*/64.

The effective focal length of a 48″ mirror with that magnification becomes 384 inches (48 × 8), which gives a moon diameter of 3.3 inches (85 mm). On a 3× enlargement of that negative you'll have a respectable view of a section of the lunar landscape.

So far the calculation was simple. But the magnification is not easy to measure accurately. To save yourself endless test shots, you may prefer approximate calculations, even though they get a bit complicated. That way, once you have the correct exposure for one magnification—for the moon or a planet, for example—you have it for all other magnifications.

For a good approximation of the magnification, measure the distance from your film to the point halfway between the lenses of the eyepiece. From that distance subtract the focal length of the eyepiece. Then divide that difference by the focal length of the eyepiece.

> EXAMPLE: You are using a ½-inch (12.5 mm) eyepiece. You measure the distance from the film to the center of the lenses of the eyepiece and get 4.5 inches (114 mm). Now $4.5 - 0.5 = 4$; $4 \div 0.5 = 8$. The magnification is $8\times$. (Metric: $114 - 12.5 = 101.5$; $101.5 \div 12.5$ is about 8.)

Instead of a regular eyepiece, you may try an achromatic Barlow as a projection lens. (Regular eyepieces are referred to as positive lenses, and the system as positive projection; a Barlow is a negative lens, the system becoming negative projection.) With a Barlow you'll get good image quality, without vignetting.

Even with a longer-focus Barlow, the length of the extension tubes will not be excessive, since the Barlow itself is *inside* the primary focus of the primary.

The f/number of this negative projection system will again be the f/number of your telescope times the magnification of your projection system. For $6\times$ magnification an f/8 telescope will give f/48. The 48-inch focal length of the primary gives an effective focal length of 288 inches (48×6). That gives a moon diameter of $2\frac{1}{4}$ inches (64 mm).

To get the approximate magnification, measure the distance from the film to the Barlow lens. Say you find 4 inches (100 mm) from some joint of the tube assembly to the lens, 6 inches (150 mm) from that joint to the film plane. The film–lens distance then is 10 inches (250 mm).

To get the approximate magnification, add the focal length of the Barlow to the film–Barlow distance. Then divide that sum by the focal length of the Barlow.

> EXAMPLE: You are using a 2-inch (50 mm) Barlow in the above example,

which gave a film–lens distance of 10 inches (250 mm). The projection magnification then is approximately $10 + 2 = 12$; $12 \div 2 = 6\times$. (Metric: $250 + 50 = 300$; $300 \div 50 = 6\times$.)

The variety of problems in astrophotography is endless.

In brightness, your objects may range from the sun to a nebula. The sun needs a filter that transmits at most $1/10{,}000$ of the light to get the exposure down to the fastest shutter speed on slow film. The nebula may be listed as magnitude 9. But that does not mean it is as bright as a ninth-magnitude star. It means that all the light that reaches us from that nebula if it were *concentrated in one point* would be as bright as such a star.

In size the targets may range from a constellation that stretches over 30 degrees to Mars, which at the most favorable opposition is not even 30 seconds in diameter. That's a ratio of $1:3600$!

The means to solve specific problems are as varied: extremely slow but fine-grained films to extra-fast films; films sensitive only in one small part of the spectrum; filters similar to those used in everyday photography; filters that pass only a very narrow band to photograph solar flares or show the fine structure of the sun's photosphere; Schmidt cameras with an f/ratio of 1.0 or better; cold cameras that use dry ice to chill the film and increase its speed; a photoelectric cell that, once locked on a guide star, keeps your telescope tracking while you watch television. . . .

Some books that will help you get started include the already mentioned *All About Telescopes* by Sam Brown (Edmund Scientific Co.); Henry E. Paul, *Outer Space Photography* (Amphoto); and George T. Keene, *Star Gazing with Telescope and Camera* (Amphoto).

Even if you had all the books and magazine articles on astrophotography, unlimited time, and money enough to buy every gadget, you'd never learn it all!

Appendix

MAG	Star	#	Constellation	RA^h	DEC^o	
0.6	Achernar	5	Eridanus	1.6	S 57	s
1.1	Acrux	30	Crux	12.4	S 63	s
1.1	Aldebaran	10	Taurus	4.6	N 16	
0.9	Altair	51	Aquila	19.8	N 9	
1.2	Antares	42	Scorpius	16.5	S 26	
0.2	Arcturus	37	Boötes	14.2	N 19	
1.4	Becrux	—	Crux	12.7	S 60	s
Var.	Betelgeuse	16	Orion	5.9	N 7	
−0.9	Canopus	17	Carina	6.4	S 53	s
0.2	Capella	12	Auriga	5.2	N 46	
1.3	Deneb	53	Cygnus	20.7	N 45	
1.3	Fomalhaut	56	Piscis Austr.	22.9	S 30	
0.9	Hadar	35	Centaurus	14.0	S 60	s
1.2	Pollux	21	Gemini	7.7	N 28	
0.5	Procyon	20	Canis Minor	7.6	N 5	
1.3	Regulus	26	Leo	10.1	N 12	
0.3	Rigel	11	Orion	5.2	S 8	
0.1	Rigil Kent	38	Centaurus	14.6	S 61	s
−1.6	Sirius	18	Canis Major	6.7	S 17	
1.2	Spica	33	Virgo	13.4	S 11	
0.1	Vega	49	Lyra	18.6	N 39	

Fig. 73. All first-magnitude stars with magnitude (Var. means variable, navagational star number, constellation, right ascension and declination.

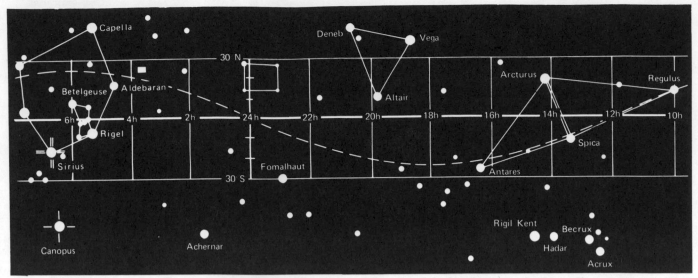

Fig. 74. Star map for stargazers in the Northern Hemisphere, including all second-magnitude stars within the strip. This strip can be used at any star time. Most stars and hour lines appear twice on the map. To align the map with the sky, use the hour line nearest the fold. The planets Mars, Jupiter, and Saturn will never be far from the dashed curve, the ecliptic.

Date		Evening Hours						Mid-night	Morning Hours					
		6	**7**	**8**	**9**	**10**	**11**		**1**	**2**	**3**	**4**	**5**	**6**
Jan.	5	1	2	3	4	5	6	7	8	9	10	11	12	13
	13	1½	2½	3½	4½	5½	6½	7½	8½	9½	10½	11½	12½	13½
	20	2	3	4	5	6	7	8	9	10	11	12	13	14
	28	2½	3½	4½	5½	6½	7½	8½	9½	10½	11½	12½	13½	14½
Feb.	4	3	4	5	6	7	8	9	10	11	12	13	14	15
	12	3½	4½	5½	6½	7½	8½	9½	10½	11½	12½	13½	14½	15½
	20	4	5	6	7	8	9	10	11	12	13	14	15	16
	27	4½	5½	6½	7½	8½	9½	10½	11½	12½	13½	14½	15½	16½
Mar.	7	5	6	7	8	9	10	11	12	13	14	15	16	17
	15	5½	6½	7½	8½	9½	10½	11½	12½	13½	14½	15½	16½	17½
	22	6	7	8	9	10	11	12	13	14	15	16	17	18
	30	6½	7½	8½	9½	10½	11½	12½	13½	14½	15½	16½	17½	18½
Apr.	7	7	8	9	10	11	12	13	14	15	16	17	18	19
	14	7½	8½	9½	10½	11½	12½	13½	14½	15½	16½	17½	18½	19½
	22	8	9	10	11	12	13	14	15	16	17	18	19	20
	29	8½	9½	10½	11½	12½	13½	14½	15½	16½	17½	18½	19½	20½
May	7	9	10	11	12	13	14	15	16	17	18	19	20	21
	15	9½	10½	11½	12½	13½	14½	15½	16½	17½	18½	19½	20½	21½
	22	10	11	12	13	14	15	16	17	18	19	20	21	22
	30	10½	11½	12½	13½	14½	15½	16½	17½	18½	19½	20½	21½	22½
June	7	11	12	13	14	15	16	17	18	19	20	21	22	23
	14	11½	12½	13½	14½	15½	16½	17½	18½	19½	20½	21½	22½	23½
	22	12	13	14	15	16	17	18	19	20	21	22	23	0
	30	12½	13½	14½	15½	16½	17½	18½	19½	20½	21½	22½	23½	½

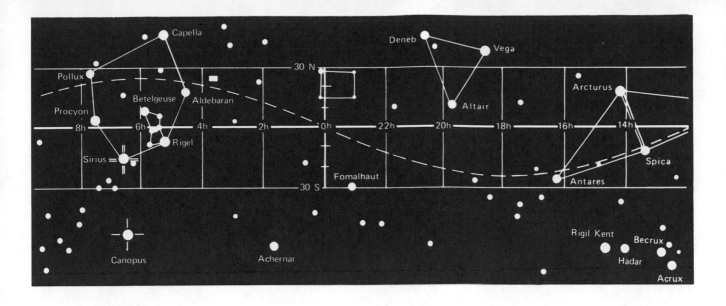

Date		Evening Hours						Mid-night	Morning Hours					
		6	7	8	9	10	11		1	2	3	4	5	6
July	7	13	14	15	16	17	18	19	20	21	22	23	0	1
	15	13½	14½	15½	16½	17½	18½	19½	20½	21½	22½	23½	½	1½
	22	14	15	16	17	18	19	20	21	22	23	0	1	2
	30	14½	15½	16½	17½	18½	19½	20½	21½	22½	23½	½	1½	2½
Aug.	7	15	16	17	18	19	20	21	22	23	0	1	2	3
	14	15½	16½	17½	18½	19½	20½	21½	22½	23½	½	1½	2½	3½
	22	16	17	18	19	20	21	22	23	0	1	2	3	4
	30	16½	17½	18½	19½	20½	21½	22½	23½	½	1½	2½	3½	4½
Sep.	7	17	18	19	20	21	22	23	0	1	2	3	4	5
	14	17½	18½	19½	20½	21½	22½	23½	½	1½	2½	3½	4½	5½
	21	18	19	20	21	22	23	0	1	2	3	4	5	6
	28	18½	19½	20½	21½	22½	23½	½	1½	2½	3½	4½	5½	6½
Oct.	6	19	20	21	22	23	0	1	2	3	4	5	6	7
	13	19½	20½	21½	22½	23½	½	1½	2½	3½	4½	5½	6½	7½
	21	20	21	22	23	0	1	2	3	4	5	6	7	8
	28	20½	21½	22½	23½	½	1½	2½	3½	4½	5½	6½	7½	8½
Nov.	5	21	22	23	0	1	2	3	4	5	6	7	8	9
	13	21½	22½	23½	½	1½	2½	3½	4½	5½	6½	7½	8½	9½
	21	22	23	0	1	2	3	4	5	6	7	8	9	10
	28	22½	23½	½	1½	2½	3½	4½	5½	6½	7½	8½	9½	10½
Dec.	6	23	0	1	2	3	4	5	6	7	8	9	10	11
	13	23½	½	1½	2½	3½	4½	5½	6½	7½	8½	9½	10½	11½
	21	0	1	2	3	4	5	6	7	8	9	10	11	12
	29	½	1½	2½	3½	4½	5½	6½	7½	8½	9½	10½	11½	12½

Fig. 75. Approximate star time from date and standard time at your location. See page 59.

Calendar

Observational data for moon and planets for naked-eye viewing or aiming a telescope equipped with setting circles

KEY

Plain figures (without decimal point, degree mark, plus or minus sign, N or S label)   Days of the month.

-o-   Planet too close to the sun for observation.

to 5   From the beginning of the month to about the fifth.

after 25   From about the twenty-fifth to the end of the month.

AM   Planet (Mercury or Venus) visible in the morning, before sunrise, in the eastern sky.

PM   Planet (Mercury or Venus) visible in the evening, after sunset, in the western sky.

RA   Right ascension, given in hours and tenths (6 minutes)—the left/right position of a planet on a star map such as Figure 11. Also the local star time when the planet is south of you (north in the Southern Hemisphere).

DEC   Declination, given to nearest whole degree—the up-and-down position of a planet on a star map such as Figure 11.

MAG   Magnitude (brightness) of planets. The lower the number, the brighter the planet appears. Minus numbers are lower than positive numbers. See also Figures 30 and 31.

BODIES

Moon Dates of phases of the moon: new for new moon, first for first quarter, full for full moon, last for last quarter. For times the moon is above the horizon, or south of you (north in the Southern Hemisphere). See pages 61–63.

Mercury Visibility AM or PM, and magnitude at the date given. When no date is given, Mercury is visible all month, the first magnitude referring to the beginning of the month, the second to the end. See also pages 51–53.

Venus Visibility AM or PM, midmonth angle from the sun, and magnitude. See also pages 48–51.

Mars RA, DEC, and MAG are given for ten-day intervals. See also pages 53–55.

Jupiter Same data as for Mars, but since they change slowly (Fig. 36), only for midmonth. See also pages 56–57.

Saturn Same data as for Mars, but since they change very slowly (Fig. 37), only for midmonth. See also pages 57–59.

Stars RA, DEC, and MAG (+1.2 for all) of five stars near the path of Mars, Jupiter, and Saturn are given at the bottom of the calendar pages, to let you compare their position and magnitude with those of the planets.

1980

JANUARY

Moon	Full 2			Last 10
	New 17			First 24
	Full 31			
Mercury	AM to 5			−0.5
Venus	PM		34°	−3.5
		RA	DEC	MAG
Mars	5	11.1	N 9	+0.2
	15	11.2	N 9	−0.1
	25	11.2	N10	−0.3
Jupiter	15	10.8	N 9	−1.9
Saturn	15	11.9	N 3	+1.1

APRIL

Moon	Last 8			New 14
	First 21			Full 30
Mercury	AM			+0.6 to −0.7
Venus	PM		45°	−4.1
		RA	DEC	MAG
Mars	5	10.0	N16	−0.2
	15	10.0	N15	−0.1
	25	10.0	N14	+0.2
Jupiter	15	10.2	N12	−1.9
Saturn	15	11.5	N 6	+0.9

FEBRUARY

Moon	Last 9			New 16
	First 23			Full 29
Mercury	PM after 5			−1.0
	-o- after 28			+1.7
Venus	PM		41°	−3.6
		RA	DEC	MAG
Mars	5	11.0	N11	−0.7
	15	10.9	N12	−0,9
	25	10.6	N13	−1.0
Jupiter	15	10.6	N10	−2.0
Saturn	15	11.8	N 4	+1.0

MAY

Moon	Last 7			New 14
	First 21			Full 29
Mercury	AM to 5			−1.2
	PM after 22			−1.5
Venus	PM		36°	−4.2
		RA	DEC	MAG
Mars	5	10.2	N13	+0.4
	15	10.4	N12	+0.6
	25	10.6	N10	+0.7
Jupiter	15	10.2	N12	−1.7
Saturn	15	11.5	N 6	+1.1

MARCH

Moon	Last 9			New 16
	First 23			Full 31
Mercury	AM after 10			+2.0
Venus	PM		45°	−3.8
		RA	DEC	MAG
Mars	5	10.4	N14	−1.0
	15	10.2	N15	−0.8
	25	10.0	N16	−0.6
Jupiter	15	10.3	N12	−2.0
Saturn	15	11.7	N 5	+0.8

JUNE

Moon	Last 5			New 12
	First 20			Full 28
Mercury	PM			−0.2 to +1.9
Venus	PM to 7			
	AM after 22			
		RA	DEC	MAG
Mars	5	10.9	N 8	+0.9
	15	11.2	N 6	+1.0
	25	11.5	N 4	+1.1
Jupiter	15	10.4	N11	−1.5
Saturn	15	11.5	N 6	+1.2

Nearby comparison stars (all of magnitude +1.2): Aldebaran 4.6^h, N16°; Pollux 7.7^h, N28°

1980

JULY

Moon	Last 5			New 12
	First 20			Full 27
Mercury	PM to 6			+2.6
	AM after 18			+2.4
Venus	AM		36°	−4.2
		RA	DEC	MAG
Mars	5	11.8	N 2	+1.2
	15	12.1	S 1	+1.2
	25	12.5	S 3	+1.3
Jupiter	15	10.7	N 9	−1.3
Saturn	15	11.6	N 5	+1.4

AUGUST

Moon	Last 3			New 10
	First 18			Full 25
Mercury	AM to 17			−1.2
Venus	AM		45°	−4.1
		RA	DEC	MAG
Mars	5	12.9	S 6	+1.4
	15	13.3	S 8	+1.4
	25	13.7	S 11	+1.5
Jupiter	15	11.1	N 7	−1.3
Saturn	15	11.8	N 4	+1.2

SEPTEMBER

Moon	Last 1			New 9
	First 17			Full 24
	Last 30			
Mercury	PM after 7			−0.7
Venus	AM		45°	−3.8
		RA	DEC	MAG
Mars	5	14.1	S 13	+1.5
	15	14.6	S 16	+1.5
	25	15.0	S 18	+1.5
Jupiter		-o-		
Saturn	-o- after 10			

OCTOBER

Moon	New 8			First 16
	Full 23			Last 30
Mercury	PM		0.0 to	+1.7
Venus	AM		41°	−3.6
		RA	DEC	MAG
Mars	5	15.5	S 20	+1.5
	15	16.0	S 21	+1.5
	25	16.5	S 23	+1.5
Jupiter	15	11.9	N 2	−1.2
Saturn	-o- to 10			
	15	12.2	N 1	+1.2

NOVEMBER

Moon	New 7			First 15
	Full 22			Last 29
Mercury	AM after 9			+1.6
Venus	AM		34°	−3.5
		RA	DEC	MAG
Mars	5	17.1	S 24	+1.5
	15	17.6	S 24	+1.5
	25	18.2	S 24	+1.4
Jupiter	15	12.2	0	−1.4
Saturn	15	12.4	S 1	+1.2

DECEMBER

Moon	New 7			First 14
	Full 21			Last 29
Mercury	AM to 13			−0.5
Venus	AM		27°	−3.4
		RA	DEC	MAG
Mars	5	18.6	S 24	+1.4
	15	19.3	S 22	+1.4
	25	19.8	S 22	+1.4
Jupiter	15	12.5	S 2	−1.5
Saturn	15	12.6	S 1	+1.1

Regulus 10.1^h, N12°; Spica 13.4^h, S11°; Antares 16.5^h, S26°

1981

JANUARY

Moon	New 6			First 13
	Full 20			Last 27
Mercury	PM after 18			−0.9
Venus	AM		20°	−3.3
		RA	DEC	MAG
Mars	5	20.4	S 20	+1.4
	15	21.0	S 18	+1.4
	25	21.5	S 16	+1.4
Jupiter	15	12.7	S 3	−1.7
Saturn	15	12.7	S 2	+1.0

APRIL

Moon	New 4			First 11
	Full 19			Last 27
Mercury	AM to 18			−1.0
Venus		-o-		
		RA	DEC	MAG
Mars			-o-	
Jupiter	15	12.2	0	−2.0
Saturn	15	12.4	0	+0.8

FEBRUARY

Moon	New 4			First 11
	Full 18			Last 26
Mercury	PM to 12			+1.5
	AM after 22			+1.8
Venus	AM to 25		13°	−3.4
		RA	DEC	MAG
Mars	5	22.1	S 13	+1.4
	-o- after 7			
Jupiter	15	12.6	S 2	−1.9
Saturn	15	12.6	S 1	+0.8

MAY

Moon	New 3			First 10
	Full 18			Last 26
Mercury	PM after 17			−1.3
Venus	PM after 16			
		RA	DEC	MAG
Mars	-o- to 17			
	25	3.3	N18	+1.6
Jupiter	15	12.1	N 1	−1.8
Saturn	15	12.1	N 1	+1.0

MARCH

Moon	New 6			First 12
	Full 20			Last 28
Mercury	AM			+1.1 to +0.4
Venus		-o-		
		RA	DEC	MAG
Mars			-o-	
Jupiter	15	12.5	S 1	−2.0
Saturn	15	12.5	0	+0.7

JUNE

Moon	New 2			First 9
	Full 17			Last 25
Mercury	PM to 16			+2.5
	AM after 29			+2.4
Venus	PM		18°	−3.3
		RA	DEC	MAG
Mars	5	3.8	N20	+1.6
	15	4.3	N22	+1.7
	25	4.8	N23	+1.7
Jupiter	15	12.1	N 1	−1.7
Saturn	15	12.2	N 1	+1.1

Nearby comparison stars (all of magnitude +1.2): Aldebaran 4.6^h, N16°; Pollux 7.7^h, N28°

1981

JULY

Moon	New 1		First 8
	Full 16		Last 24
	New 30		
Mercury	AM		+2.0 to −1.2
Venus	PM	26°	−3.3

Mars		RA	DEC	MAG
	5	5.3	N23	+1.7
	15	5.8	N24	+1.7
	25	6.3	N24	+1.8
Jupiter	15	12.3	0	−1.5
Saturn	15	12.3	0	+1.2

OCTOBER

Moon	First 6		Full 13
	Last 19		New 27
Mercury	PM to 14		+2.3
	AM after 24		+1.5
Venus	PM	45°	−3.8

Mars		RA	DEC	MAG
	5	9.5	N16	+1.7
	15	9.9	N14	+1.7
	25	10.3	N12	+1.6
Jupiter		-o-		
Saturn	-o- to 20			

AUGUST

Moon	First 7		Full 15
	Last 22		New 29
Mercury	PM after 20		−0.8
Venus	PM	33°	−3.4

Mars		RA	DEC	MAG
	5	6.9	N24	+1.8
	15	7.3	N23	+1.8
	25	7.6	N22	+1.8
Jupiter	15	12.5	S 2	−1.3
Saturn	15	12.5	S 1	+1.2

NOVEMBER

Moon	First 4		Full 11
	Last 18		New 26
Mercury	AM to 21		−0.7
Venus	PM	47°	−4.1

Mars		RA	DEC	MAG
	5	10.7	N10	+1.6
	15	11.1	N 8	+1.5
	25	11.4	N 6	+1.4
Jupiter	15	13.7	S 10	−1.2
Saturn	15	13.1	S 5	+1.0

SEPTEMBER

Moon	First 6		Full 13
	Last 20		New 27
Mercury	PM to 30		+0.5
Venus	PM	40°	−3.5

Mars		RA	DEC	MAG
	5	8.3	N21	+1.8
	15	8.7	N19	+1.8
	25	9.1	N18	+1.7
Jupiter	15	12.9	S 5	−1.2
Saturn	15	12.7	S 2	+1.1
	-o- after 25			

DECEMBER

Moon	First 4		Full 11
	Last 18		New 26
Mercury	PM after 28		−0.7
Venus	PM	41°	−4.4

Mars		RA	DEC	MAG
	5	11.7	N 4	+1.3
	15	12.0	N 2	+1.2
	25	12.3	0	+1.1
Jupiter	15	14.1	S 11	−1.3
Saturn	15	13.3	S 6	+1.0

Regulus 10.1^h, N12°; Spica 13.4^h, S11°; Antares 16.5^h, S26°

1982

JANUARY

Moon	First 2			Full 9
	Last 16			New 24
Mercury	PM to 27			+1.2
Venus	PM to 15			−3.4
	AM after 26			

		RA	DEC	MAG
Mars	5	12.6	S 1	+0.8
	15	12.8	S 3	+0.6
	25	13.0	S 4	+0.4
Jupiter	15	14.4	S 13	−1.5
Saturn	15	13.4	S 6	+0.9

FEBRUARY

Moon	First 1			Full 8
	Last 15			New 23
Mercury	AM after 6			+1.8
Venus	AM		33°	−4.3

		RA	DEC	MAG
Mars	5	13.2	S 4	+0.2
	15	13.2	S 5	−0.1
	25	13.2	S 5	−0.3
Jupiter	15	14.5	S 14	−1.7
Saturn	15	13.4	S 6	+0.8

MARCH

Moon	First 2			Full 9
	Last 17			New 25
Mercury	AM			+0.3 to −0.7
Venus	AM		45°	−4.2

		RA	DEC	MAG
Mars	5	13.2	S 4	−0.5
	15	13.0	S 3	−0.8
	25	12.9	S 2	−1.0
Jupiter	15	14.5	S 13	−1.9
Saturn	15	13.3	S 5	+0.6

APRIL

Moon	First 1			Full 8
	Last 16			New 23
	First 30			
Mercury	PM after 22			−1.1
Venus	AM		46°	−3.9

		RA	DEC	MAG
Mars	5	12.6	S 1	−1.2
	15	12.4	0	−1.1
	25	12.2	N 1	−0.9
Jupiter	15	14.3	S 12	−2.0
Saturn	15	13.2	S 5	+0.5

MAY

Moon	Full 7			Last 16
	New 22			First 29
Mercury	PM to 25			+2.3
Venus	AM		42°	−3.6

		RA	DEC	MAG
Mars	5	12.1	N 1	−0.6
	15	12.1	N 1	−0.4
	25	12.1	0	−0.2
Jupiter	15	14.1	S 11	−2.0
Saturn	15	13.1	S 4	+0.7

JUNE

Moon	Full 6			Last 14
	New 21			First 28
Mercury	AM after 9			+2.6
Venus	AM		36°	−3.4

		RA	DEC	MAG
Mars	5	12.2	S 1	0.0
	15	12.4	S 3	+0.2
	25	12.6	S 4	+0.3
Jupiter	15	13.9	S 10	−1.9
Saturn	15	13.0	S 4	+0.9

Nearby comparison stars (all of magnitude +1.2): Aldebaran 4.6^h, N16°; Pollux 7.7^h, N28°

1982

JULY

Moon	Full 6		Last 13
	New 20		First 27
Mercury	AM to 16		−1.3
Venus	AM	29°	−3.3

		RA	DEC	MAG
Mars	5	12.9	S 5	+0.5
	15	13.2	S 8	+0.6
	25	13.5	S 10	+0.7
Jupiter	15	13.9	S 11	−1.7
Saturn	15	13.0	S 4	+1.0

OCTOBER

Moon	Full 2		Last 9
	New 16		First 24
Mercury	AM after 8		+1.5
Venus		-o-	

		RA	DEC	MAG
Mars	5	16.6	S 23	+1.1
	15	17.1	S 24	+1.1
	25	17.6	S 25	+1.1
Jupiter	15	14.8	S 15	−1.3
Saturn	-o- after 8		

AUGUST

Moon	Full 4		Last 12
	New 18		First 26
Mercury	PM after 5		−0.8
Venus	AM	21°	−3.3

		RA	DEC	MAG
Mars	5	13.9	S 13	+0.8
	15	14.3	S 15	+0.9
	25	14.7	S 17	+0.9
Jupiter	15	14.1	S 12	−1.5
Saturn	15	13.2	S 5	+1.1

NOVEMBER

Moon	Full 1		Last 8
	New 15		First 23
	Full 30		
Mercury	AM to 3		−0.9
Venus		-o-	

		RA	DEC	MAG
Mars	5	18.2	S 25	+1.2
	15	18.8	S 24	+1.2
	25	19.3	S 24	+1.2
Jupiter		-o-	
Saturn	15	13.8	S 9	+0.9

SEPTEMBER

Moon	Full 3		Last 10
	New 17		First 24
Mercury	PM to 27		+1.9
Venus	AM to 28	13°	−3.4

		RA	DEC	MAG
Mars	5	15.1	S 19	+1.0
	15	15.6	S 21	+1.0
	25	16.1	S 22	+1.1
Jupiter	15	14.4	S 13	−1.3
Saturn	15	13.4	S 6	+1.0

DECEMBER

Moon	Last 8		New 15
	First 23		Full 30
Mercury	PM after 8		−0.6
Venus	PM after 13	11°	−3.4

		RA	DEC	MAG
Mars	5	19.9	S 22	+1.3
	15	20.4	S 21	+1.3
	25	20.9	S 19	+1.3
Jupiter	15	15.7	S 19	−1.3
Saturn	15	14.0	S 10	+0.9

Regulus 10.1^h, N12°; Spica 13.4^h, S11°; Antares 16.5^h, S26°

1983

JANUARY

Moon	Last 5			New 14
	First 22			Full 28
Mercury	PM to 11			+1.4
	AM after 21			+1.6
Venus	PM		18°	−3.3
		RA	DEC	MAG
Mars	5	21.5	S 16	+1.3
	15	22.0	S 13	+1.4
	25	22.5	S 10	+1.4
Jupiter	15	16.1	S 20	−1.4
Saturn	15	14.1	S 10	+0.8

FEBRUARY

Moon	Last 4			New 12
	First 20			Full 27
Mercury	AM			+0.4 to −0.1
Venus	PM		25°	−3.4
		RA	DEC	MAG
Mars	5	23.0	S 7	+1.4
	15	23.5	S 4	+1.4
	25	0.0	S 1	+1.5
Jupiter	15	16.5	S 21	−1.6
Saturn	15	14.2	S 10	+0.7

MARCH

Moon	Last 6			New 14
	First 21			Full 28
Mercury	AM to 15			−0.7
Venus	PM		31°	−3.4
		RA	DEC	MAG
Mars	5	0.4	N 2	+1.5
	15	0.8	N 5	+1.5
	25	1.3	N 8	+1.5
Jupiter	15	16.6	S 21	−1.8
Saturn	15	14.1	S 10	+0.5

APRIL

Moon	Last 5			New 13
	First 20			Full 27
Mercury	PM after 6			−1.3
Venus	PM		31°	−3.5
		RA	DEC	MAG
Mars	5	1.8	N11	+1.6
	15	2.3	N14	+1.6
	25	2.6	N16	+1.6
Jupiter	15	16.6	S 21	−2.0
Saturn	15	14.0	S 9	+0.4

MAY

Moon	Last 4			New 12
	First 19			Full 26
Mercury	PM to 6			+2.4
	AM after 19			+2.6
Venus	PM		43°	−3.7
		RA	DEC	MAG
Mars		-o-		
Jupiter	15	16.4	S 21	−2.1
Saturn	15	13.9	S 9	+0.5

JUNE

Moon	Last 3			New 10
	First 17			Full 25
Mercury	AM			+1.2 to −1.2
Venus	PM		45°	−3.9
		RA	DEC	MAG
Mars		-o-		
Jupiter	15	16.1	S 20	−2.1
Saturn	15	13.8	S 8	+0.7

Nearby comparison stars (all of magnitude +1.2): Aldebaran 4.6^h, N16°; Pollux 7.7^h, N28°

1983

JULY

Moon	Last 3			New 10
	First 16			Full 24
Mercury	PM after 18			−1.0
Venus	PM		41°	−4.2
		RA	DEC	MAG
Mars	-o- to 14			
	15	6.8	N24	+1.8
	25	7.3	N23	+1.9
Jupiter	15	16.0	S 20	−2.0
Saturn	15	13.8	S 8	+0.9

AUGUST

Moon	Last 1			New 8
	First 15			Full 23
	Last 31			
Mercury	PM			0.0 to +1.0
Venus	PM to 21		18°	−3.7
		RA	DEC	MAG
Mars	5	7.8	N22	+1.9
	15	8.2	N21	+1.9
	25	8.7	N20	+1.9
Jupiter	15	16.0	S 20	−1.8
Saturn	15	13.9	S 9	+0.9

SEPTEMBER

Moon	New 6			First 13
	Full 22			Last 29
Mercury	PM to 10			+2.1
	AM after 21			+1.9
Venus	AM		29°	−4.2
		RA	DEC	MAG
Mars	5	9.1	N18	+2.0
	15	9.6	N16	+2.0
	25	10.0	N14	+2.0
Jupiter	15	16.2	S 20	−1.6
Saturn	15	14.0	S 10	+0.9

OCTOBER

Moon	New 6			First 13
	Full 21			Last 28
Mercury	AM to 17			−1.0
Venus	AM		44°	−4.2
		RA	DEC	MAG
Mars	5	10.4	N12	+1.9
	15	10.7	N 9	+1.9
	25	11.1	N 7	+1.9
Jupiter	15	16.5	S 21	−1.4
Saturn	15	14.2	S 11	+0.8
	-o- after 20			

NOVEMBER

Moon	New 4			First 12
	Full 20			Last 27
Mercury	PM after 17			−0.5
Venus	AM		46°	−3.9
		RA	DEC	MAG
Mars	5	11.5	N 5	+1.9
	15	11.9	N 2	+1.8
	25	12.3	0	+1.7
Jupiter	15	16.9	S 22	−1.4
Saturn	-o- to 11			
	15	14.5	S 12	+0.8

DECEMBER

Moon	New 4			First 12
	Full 19			Last 26
Mercury	PM to 27			+1.6
Venus	AM		42°	−3.7
		RA	DEC	MAG
Mars	5	12.6	S 2	+1.7
	15	13.0	S 4	+1.6
	25	13.3	S 7	+1.5
Jupiter		-o-		
Saturn	15	14.7	S 13	+0.8

Regulus 10.1^h, N12°; Spica 13.4^h, S11°; Antares 16.5^h, S26°

The Stargazer's Bible

1984

JANUARY

Moon	New 3			First 11
	Full 18			Last 24
Mercury	AM after 4			+1.7
Venus	AM		37°	−3.5
		RA	DEC	MAG
Mars	5	13.7	S 9	+1.3
	15	14.0	S 11	+1.2
	25	14.3	S 12	+1.0
Jupiter	15	17.9	S 23	−1.4
Saturn	15	14.9	S 14	+0.8

FEBRUARY

Moon	New 1			First 9
	Full 16			Last 23
Mercury	AM to 26			−0.6
Venus	AM		31°	−3.4
		RA	DEC	MAG
Mars	5	14.7	S 14	+0.8
	15	15.0	S 15	+0.6
	25	15.2	S 16	+0.4
Jupiter	15	18.4	S 23	−1.5
Saturn	15	15.0	S 14	+0.7

MARCH

Moon	New 2			First 10
	Full 16			Last 23
Mercury	PM after 19			−1.3
Venus	AM		24°	−3.3
		RA	DEC	MAG
Mars	5	15.4	S 17	+0.2
	15	15.6	S 18	−0.1
	25	15.7	S 18	−0.3
Jupiter	15	18.7	S 23	−1.6
Saturn	15	15.0	S 14	+0.5

APRIL

Moon	New 1			First 9
	Full 15			Last 22
	New 30			
Mercury	PM to 15			+2.1
	AM after 28			+2.6
Venus	AM		15°	−3.3
		RA	DEC	MAG
Mars	5	15.8	S 19	−0.6
	15	15.7	S 19	−1.0
	25	15.6	S 19	−1.2
Jupiter	15	18.9	S 23	−1.8
Saturn	15	14.9	S 14	+0.4

MAY

Moon	First 8			Full 14
	Last 22			New 30
Mercury	AM			+2.2 to +0.1
Venus	AM to 10			
		RA	DEC	MAG
Mars	5	15.4	S 18	−1.5
	15	15.1	S 18	−1.6
	25	14.9	S 17	−1.6
Jupiter	15	18.9	S 23	−2.1
Saturn	15	14.7	S 13	+0.4

JUNE

Moon	First 6			Full 13
	Last 21			New 28
Mercury	AM to 15			−1.3
Venus			-o-	
		RA	DEC	MAG
Mars	5	14.7	S 17	−1.4
	15	14.6	S 17	−1.2
	25	14.6	S 17	−1.0
Jupiter	15	18.7	S 23	−2.2
Saturn	15	14.6	S 13	+0.5

Nearby comparison stars (all of magnitude +1.2): Aldebaran 4.6ʰ, N16°; Pollux 7.7ʰ, N28°

1984

JULY

Moon	First 5			Full 13
	Last 20			New 28
Mercury	PM			−1.2 to +0.6
Venus	PM after 21			

		RA	DEC	MAG
Mars	5	14.7	S 18	−0.8
	15	14.8	S 19	−0.6
	25	15.1	S 20	−0.4
Jupiter	15	18.5	S 23	−2.2
Saturn	15	14.5	S 12	+0.7

OCTOBER

Moon	First 1			Full 9
	Last 17			New 24
	First 31			
Mercury	PM after 27			−0.5
Venus	PM		32°	−3.4

		RA	DEC	MAG
Mars	5	18.0	S 26	+0.5
	15	18.5	S 25	+0.6
	25	19.0	S 25	+0.7
Jupiter	15	18.5	S 23	−1.7
Saturn	15	14.9	S 15	+0.8

AUGUST

Moon	First 3			Full 11
	Last 19			New 26
Mercury	PM to 23			+2.2
Venus	PM		16°	−3.3

		RA	DEC	MAG
Mars	5	15.4	S 21	−0.2
	15	15.7	S 22	0.0
	25	16.0	S 23	+0.1
Jupiter	15	18.2	S 23	−2.1
Saturn	15	14.6	S 13	+0.8

NOVEMBER

Moon	Full 8			Last 16
	New 22			First 30
Mercury	PM			−0.4 to 0.0
Venus	PM		39°	−3.5

		RA	DEC	MAG
Mars	5	19.6	S 23	+0.7
	15	20.1	S 22	+0.8
	25	20.6	S 21	+0.9
Jupiter	15	18.8	S 23	−1.6
Saturn	-o- to 21			

SEPTEMBER

Moon	First 2			Full 10
	Last 18			New 24
Mercury	AM after 4			+1.8
	-o- after 28			−1.1
Venus	PM		25°	−3.3

		RA	DEC	MAG
Mars	5	16.5	S 24	+0.2
	15	17.0	S 25	+0.3
	25	17.5	S 26	+0.4
Jupiter	15	18.2	S 23	−1.9
Saturn	15	14.7	S 14	+0.9

DECEMBER

Moon	Full 8			Last 15
	New 22			First 30
Mercury	PM to 8			+1.1
	AM after 19			+1.8
Venus	PM		44°	−3.7

		RA	DEC	MAG
Mars	5	21.2	S 18	+0.9
	15	21.7	S 15	+1.0
	25	22.2	S 13	+1.1
Jupiter	15	19.3	S 23	−1.5
Saturn	15	15.4	S 17	+0.8

Regulus 10.1^h, N12°; Spica 13.4^h, S11°; Antares 16.5^h, S26°

1985

JANUARY

Moon	Full 6			Last 13
	New 20			First 28
Mercury	AM		−0.1 to −0.4	
Venus	PM	47°	−4.0	

Mars		RA	DEC	MAG
	5	22.7	S 10	+1.2
	15	23.1	S 6	+1.2
	25	23.6	S 3	+1.3
Jupiter		-o-		
Saturn	15	15.6	S 17	+0.8

FEBRUARY

Moon	Full 5			Last 12
	New 19			First 27
Mercury	AM to 5		−0.5	
Venus	PM	45°	−4.3	

Mars		RA	DEC	MAG
	5	0.1	0	+1.4
	15	0.6	N 3	+1.4
	25	1.0	N 6	+1.5
Jupiter	15	20.3	S 20	−1.5
Saturn	15	15.7	S 18	+0.7

MARCH

Moon	Full 6			Last 13
	New 21			First 29
Mercury	PM after 3		−1.2	
Venus	PM	28°	−4.1	

Mars		RA	DEC	MAG
	5	1.4	N 9	+1.5
	15	1.8	N11	+1.6
	25	2.3	N14	+1.6
Jupiter	15	20.7	S 19	−1.6
Saturn	15	15.8	S 18	+0.5

APRIL

Moon	Full 5			Last 11
	New 20			First 27
Mercury	AM after 10		+2.3	
Venus	AM after 8	18°	−3.7	

Mars		RA	DEC	MAG
	5	2.8	N17	+1.7
	15	3.3	N19	+1.7
	25	3.8	N20	+1.8
Jupiter	15	21.0	S 17	−1.7
Saturn	15	15.7	S 17	+0.4

MAY

Moon	Full 4			Last 11
	New 19			First 27
Mercury	AM		+0.7 to −1.2	
Venus	AM	41°	−4.2	

Mars		RA	DEC	MAG
	5	4.3	N22	+1.8
	15	4.7	N23	+1.8
	25	5.2	N24	+1.8
Jupiter	15	21.3	S 17	−2.0
Saturn	15	15.5	S 17	+0.2

JUNE

Moon	Full 2			Last 10
	New 18			First 25
Mercury	PM after 16		−1.2	
Venus	AM	46°	−3.9	

Mars		RA	DEC	MAG
	5	5.8	N24	+1.9
	-o- after 14			
Jupiter	15	21.3	S 16	−2.2
Saturn	15	15.4	S 16	+0.4

Nearby comparison stars (all of magnitude +1.2): Aldebaran 4.6^h, N16°; Pollux 7.7^h, N28°

1985

JULY

Moon	Full 2			Last 9
	New 17			First 24
	Full 31			
Mercury	PM			0.0 to +1.2
Venus	AM		43°	−3.7
		RA	DEC	MAG
Mars		-o-		
Jupiter	15	21.1	S 17	−2.3
Saturn	15	15.3	S 16	+0.6

AUGUST

Moon	Last 8			New 16
	First 22			Full 30
Mercury	PM to 5			+2.3
	AM after 16			+2.3
Venus	AM		38°	−3.5
		RA	DEC	MAG
Mars	-o- to 22			
	25	9.5	N16	+2.0
Jupiter	15	20.9	S 18	−2.3
Saturn	15	15.3	S 16	+0.8

SEPTEMBER

Moon	Last 7			New 14
	First 21			Full 28
Mercury	AM to 12			−1.2
Venus	AM		30°	−3.4
		RA	DEC	MAG
Mars	5	10.0	N14	+2.0
	15	10.4	N11	+2.0
	25	10.8	N 9	+2.0
Jupiter	15	20.7	S 19	−2.3
Saturn	15	15.4	S 17	+0.8

OCTOBER

Moon	Last 7			New 13
	First 20			Full 28
Mercury	PM after 7			−0.5
Venus	AM		23°	−3.4
		RA	DEC	MAG
Mars	5	11.1	N 7	+2.0
	15	11.5	N 4	+2.0
	25	11.9	N 2	+2.0
Jupiter	15	20.7	S 19	−2.1
Saturn	15	15.6	S 18	+0.8

NOVEMBER

Moon	Last 5			New 12
	First 19			Full 27
Mercury	PM to 24			+1.5
Venus	AM		16°	−3.4
		RA	DEC	MAG
Mars	5	12.3	S 1	+2.0
	15	12.7	S 3	+1.9
	25	13.1	S 6	+1.9
Jupiter	15	20.8	S 19	−1.9
Saturn	-o- after 12			

DECEMBER

Moon	Last 5			New 11
	First 18			Full 27
Mercury	AM after 3			+1.6
Venus	AM to 11			
		RA	DEC	MAG
Mars	5	13.5	S 8	+1.9
	15	13.9	S 10	+1.8
	25	14.3	S 13	+1.7
Jupiter	15	21.2	S 17	−1.7
Saturn	-o- to 5			
	15	16.1	S 19	+0.7

Regulus 10.1^h, N12°; Spica 13.4^h, S11°; Antares 16.5^h, S26°

1986

JANUARY

Moon	Last 3			New 10
	First 17			Full 25
Mercury	AM to 15			−0.5
Venus	-o-			

		RA	DEC	MAG
Mars	5	14.7	S 15	+1.4
	15	15.1	S 17	+1.3
	25	15.5	S 18	+1.3
Jupiter	15	21.6	S 15	−1.6
Saturn	15	16.3	S 20	+0.8

FEBRUARY

Moon	Last 1			New 8
	First 16			Full 24
Mercury	PM after 14			−1.1
Venus	-o-			

		RA	DEC	MAG
Mars	5	16.0	S 20	+1.1
	15	16.4	S 21	+1.0
	25	16.8	S 22	+1.0
Jupiter	-o-			
Saturn	15	16.5	S 20	+0.6

MARCH

Moon	Last 3			New 10
	First 18			Full 25
Mercury	PM to 11			+1.8
	AM after 23			+2.1
Venus	PM		13°	−3.4

		RA	DEC	MAG
Mars	5	17.1	S 22	+0.7
	15	17.5	S 23	+0.5
	25	17.9	S 23	+0.3
Jupiter	15	22.5	S 10	−1.6
Saturn	15	16.5	S 20	+0.6

APRIL

Moon	Last 1			New 9
	First 17			Full 24
	Last 30			
Mercury	AM			+1.1 to 0.0
Venus	PM		21°	−3.3

		RA	DEC	MAG
Mars	5	18.3	S 23	+0.2
	15	18.6	S 24	0.0
	25	18.9	S 24	−0.2
Jupiter	15	22.9	S 8	−1.6
Saturn	15	16.5	S 20	+0.4

MAY

Moon	New 8			First 16
	Full 23			Last 30
Mercury	AM to 14			−1.1
Venus	PM		28°	−3.4

		RA	DEC	MAG
Mars	5	19.2	S 24	−0.5
	15	19.4	S 24	−0.8
	25	19.6	S 24	−1.2
Jupiter	15	23.3	S 6	−1.8
Saturn	15	16.4	S 20	+0.2

JUNE

Moon	New 7			First 15
	Full 21			Last 28
Mercury	PM			−1.2 to +1.0
Venus	PM		34°	−3.4

		RA	DEC	MAG
Mars	5	19.7	S 25	−1.5
	15	19.7	S 25	−1.8
	25	19.6	S 26	−2.1
Jupiter	15	23.5	S 4	−2.0
Saturn	15	16.2	S 19	+0.3

Nearby comparison stars (all of magnitude +1.2): Aldebaran 4.6h, N16°; Pollux 7.7h, N28°

1986

JULY

Moon	New 6			First 14
	Full 21			Last 28
Mercury	PM to 18			+2.5
	AM after 29			+2.3
Venus	PM		41°	−3.6
		RA	DEC	MAG
Mars	5	19.4	S 27	−2.3
	15	19.2	S 27	−2.4
	25	19.0	S 29	−2.3
Jupiter	15	23.6	S 4	−2.2
Saturn	15	16.1	S 19	+0.5

AUGUST

Moon	New 5			First 12
	Full 19			Last 27
Mercury	AM to 27			−1.2
Venus	PM		45°	−3.8
		RA	DEC	MAG
Mars	5	18.9	S 29	−2.0
	15	18.9	S 28	−1.8
	25	18.9	S 28	−1.5
Jupiter	15	23.5	S 5	−2.4
Saturn	15	16.1	S 19	+0.7

SEPTEMBER

Moon	New 4			First 11
	Full 18			Last 25
Mercury	PM after 18			−0.8
Venus	PM		44°	−4.2
		RA	DEC	MAG
Mars	5	19.1	S 27	−1.3
	15	19.4	S 26	−1.1
	25	19.7	S 25	−0.8
Jupiter	15	23.3	S 6	−2.4
Saturn	15	16.2	S 19	+0.8

OCTOBER

Moon	New 3			First 10
	Full 17			Last 25
Mercury	PM			−0.1 to +0.5
Venus	PM		44°	−4.2
		RA	DEC	MAG
Mars	5	20.0	S 24	−0.6
	15	20.4	S 22	−0.4
	25	20.8	S 20	−0.3
Jupiter	15	23.0	S 8	−2.3
Saturn	15	16.3	S 20	+0.8

NOVEMBER

Moon	New 2			First 8
	Full 16			Last 24
Mercury	PM to 8			+1.8
	AM after 18			+2.2
Venus	PM		30°	−4.1
		RA	DEC	MAG
Mars	5	21.3	S 18	−0.1
	15	21.7	S 16	+0.1
	25	22.1	S 13	+0.2
Jupiter	15	23.0	S 8	−2.2
Saturn	15	16.6	S 20	+0.7
	-o- after 23			

DECEMBER

Moon	New 1			First 8
	Full 16			Last 24
	New 30			
Mercury	AM to 26			−0.5
Venus	AM after 11		16°	−3.7
		RA	DEC	MAG
Mars	5	22.5	S 10	+0.4
	15	23.0	S 8	+0.5
	25	23.4	S 5	+0.7
Jupiter	15	23.1	S 7	−2.0
Saturn	-o- to 16			

Regulus 10.1^h, N12°; Spica 13.4^h, S11°; Antares 16.5^h, S26°

1987

JANUARY

Moon	First 6			Full 14
	Last 22			New 29
Mercury	PM after 29			−1.0
Venus	AM		47°	−4.1
		RA	DEC	MAG
Mars	5	23.9	S 1	+0.8
	15	0.3	N 2	+0.9
	25	0.7	N 5	+1.0
Jupiter	15	23.4	S 5	−1.8
Saturn	15	17.1	S 21	+0.7

FEBRUARY

Moon	First 5			Full 13
	Last 21			New 28
Mercury	PM to 22			+1.7
Venus	AM		45°	−3.8
		RA	DEC	MAG
Mars	5	1.2	N 8	+1.2
	15	1.6	N10	+1.3
	25	2.0	N13	+1.4
Jupiter	15	23.8	S 2	−1.6
Saturn	15	17.2	S 22	+0.7

MARCH

Moon	First 7			Full 15
	Last 22			New 29
Mercury	AM after 5			+2.1
Venus	AM		40°	−3.6
		RA	DEC	MAG
Mars	5	2.4	N15	+1.4
	15	2.8	N17	+1.5
	25	3.3	N19	+1.6
Jupiter	-o- after 10			
Saturn	15	17.3	S 22	+0.7

APRIL

Moon	First 6			Full 13
	Last 20			New 27
Mercury	AM to 29			−1.0
Venus	AM		34°	−3.4
		RA	DEC	MAG
Mars	5	3.8	N21	+1.7
	15	4.3	N22	+1.7
	25	4.8	N23	+1.8
Jupiter	-o- to 11			
	15	0.7	N 3	−1.8
Saturn	15	17.3	S 22	+0.5

MAY

Moon	First 5			Full 13
	Last 19			New 27
Mercury	PM after 16			−1.3
Venus	AM		27°	−3.3
		RA	DEC	MAG
Mars	5	5.2	N24	+1.8
	15	5.7	N24	+1.8
	25	6.2	N25	+1.9
Jupiter	15	1.1	N 6	−1.7
Saturn	15	17.2	N21	+0.4

JUNE

Moon	First 4			Full 11
	Last 18			New 26
Mercury	PM to 28			+2.6
Venus	AM		19°	−3.3
		RA	DEC	MAG
Mars	5	6.7	N24	+2.0
	15	7.2	N24	+2.0
	25	7.6	N23	+2.0
Jupiter	15	1.5	N 8	−1.8
Saturn	15	17.1	S 21	+0.2

Nearby comparison stars (all of magnitude +1.2): Aldebaran 4.6^h, N16°; Pollux 7.7^h, N28°

1987

JULY

Moon	First 4			Full 10
	Last 17			New 25
Mercury	AM after 10			+2.4
Venus	AM	11°		−3.4
	-o- after 19			

	RA	DEC	MAG
Mars	5	8.1	N22	+2.0
	15	8.5	N20	+2.0
	-o- after 24		
Jupiter	15	1.7	N 9	−2.0
Saturn	15	17.0	S 21	+0.4

OCTOBER

Moon	Full 6			Last 14
	New 22			First 29
Mercury	PM to 23			+1.8
Venus	PM	15°		−3.3

	RA	DEC	MAG
Mars	5	11.9	N 2	+2.0
	15	12.3	S 1	+2.0
	25	12.7	S 3	+2.0
Jupiter	15	1.6	N 8	−2.5
Saturn	15	17.1	S 22	+0.8

AUGUST

Moon	First 2			Full 9
	Last 16			New 24
	First 31			
Mercury	AM to 11			−1.2
Venus		-o-		

	RA	DEC	MAG
Mars		-o-		
Jupiter	15	1.9	N10	−2.2
Saturn	15	16.9	S 21	+0.6

NOVEMBER

Moon	Full 5			Last 13
	New 21			First 27
Mercury	AM after 3			+1.2
Venus	PM	22°		−3.3

	RA	DEC	MAG
Mars	5	13.1	S 6	+2.0
	15	13.5	S 9	+2.0
	25	13.9	S 11	+1.9
Jupiter	15	1.4	N 7	−2.4
Saturn	15	17.3	S 22	+0.7

SEPTEMBER

Moon	Full 7		Last 14
	New 22		First 30
Mercury	PM		−0.8 to +0.2
Venus		-o-	

	RA	DEC	MAG
Mars	-o- to 24		
	25	11.5	N 4	+2.0
Jupiter	15	1.8	N 9	−2.4
Saturn	15	16.9	S 21	+0.7

DECEMBER

Moon	Full 5			Last 13
	New 20			First 27
Mercury	AM to 6			−0.6
Venus	PM	29°		−3.4

	RA	DEC	MAG
Mars	5	14.3	S 13	+1.9
	15	14.8	S 15	+1.8
	25	15.2	S 17	+1.8
Jupiter	15	1.2	N 6	−2.2
Saturn	-o- 5 to 24		

Regulus 10.1^h, N12°; Spica 13.4^h, S11°; Antares 16.5^h, S26°

1988

JANUARY

Moon	Full 3			Last 12
	New 19			First 25
Mercury	PM after 9			−0.8
Venus	PM		35°	−3.5
		RA	DEC	MAG
Mars	5	15.7	S 19	+1.7
	15	16.1	S 21	+1.6
	25	16.6	S 22	+1.5
Jupiter	15	1.3	N 7	−2.0
Saturn	15	17.8	S 22	+0.7

FEBRUARY

Moon	Full 2			Last 10
	New 17			First 24
Mercury	PM to 6			+1.7
	AM after 16			+1.7
Venus	PM		41°	−3.6
		RA	DEC	MAG
Mars	5	17.1	S 23	+1.4
	15	17.6	S 23	+1.4
	25	18.1	S 24	+1.3
Jupiter	15	1.6	N 9	−1.8
Saturn	15	18.0	S 22	+0.8

MARCH

Moon	Full 3			Last 11
	New 17			First 24
Mercury	AM		+0.6 to −0.2	
Venus	PM		45°	−3.8
		RA	DEC	MAG
Mars	5	18.6	S 24	+1.2
	15	19.0	S 23	+1.1
	25	19.5	S 22	+1.0
Jupiter	15	2.0	N11	−1.7
Saturn	15	18.1	S 22	+0.7

APRIL

Moon	Full 2			Last 9
	New 16			First 23
Mercury	AM to 10			−0.9
	PM after 29			−1.4
Venus	PM		45°	−4.1
		RA	DEC	MAG
Mars	5	20.1	S 21	+0.8
	15	20.5	S 20	+0.7
	25	21.0	S 19	+0.6
Jupiter	15	2.4	N13	−1.6
	-o- after 19			
Saturn	15	18.2	S 22	+0.6

MAY

Moon	Full 1			Last 8
	New 15			First 23
	Full 31			
Mercury	PM		−1.2 to +1.8	
Venus	PM		36°	−4.2
		RA	DEC	MAG
Mars	5	21.5	S 17	+0.4
	15	21.9	S 15	+0.3
	25	22.3	S 13	+0.1
Jupiter	-o- to 14			
	15	2.9	N16	−1.6
Saturn	15	18.1	S 22	+0.5

JUNE

Moon	Last 7			New 14
	First 22			Full 29
Mercury	PM to 6			+2.3
	AM after 20			+2.3
Venus	PM to 6			
	AM after 21			
		RA	DEC	MAG
Mars	5	22.7	S 11	−0.1
	15	23.1	S 9	−0.3
	25	23.5	S 7	−0.5
Jupiter	15	3.4	N18	−1.6
Saturn	15	18.0	S 22	+0.2

Nearby comparison stars (all of magnitude +1.2): Aldebaran 4.6^h, N16°; Pollux 7.7^h, N28°

1988

JULY

Moon	Last 6			New 13
	First 21			Full 28
Mercury	AM to 25			−1.3
Venus	AM		36°	−4.2
		RA	DEC	MAG
Mars	5	23.8	S 5	−0.7
	15	0.1	S 3	−1.0
	25	0.4	S 2	−1.2
Jupiter	15	3.8	N19	−1.7
Saturn	15	17.8	S 22	+0.4

OCTOBER

Moon	Last 2			New 10
	First 18			Full 24
Mercury	PM to 6			+1.8
	AM after 16			+1.7
Venus	AM		40°	−3.6
		RA	DEC	MAG
Mars	5	0.3	S 2	−2.4
	15	0.2	S 3	−2.1
	25	0.1	S 2	−1.8
Jupiter	15	4.3	N20	−2.3
Saturn	15	17.8	S 23	+0.7

AUGUST

Moon	Last 4			New 12
	First 20			Full 27
Mercury	PM after 13			−0.8
Venus	AM		46°	−4.0
		RA	DEC	MAG
Mars	5	0.6	S 1	−1.5
	15	0.8	0	−1.7
	25	0.8	0	−2.0
Jupiter	15	4.1	N20	−1.9
Saturn	15	17.7	S 22	+0.5

NOVEMBER

Moon	Last 1			New 9
	First 16			Full 23
Mercury	AM to 15			−0.8
Venus	AM		33°	−3.5
		RA	DEC	MAG
Mars	5	0.1	S 2	−1.5
	15	0.2	0	−1.2
	25	0.3	N 1	−0.8
Jupiter	15	4.0	N20	−2.4
Saturn	15	18.0	S 23	+0.7

SEPTEMBER

Moon	Last 3			New 10
	First 18			Full 25
Mercury	PM			+0.1 to +1.1
Venus	AM		44°	−3.8
		RA	DEC	MAG
Mars	5	0.8	S 1	−2.2
	15	0.7	S 1	−2.4
	25	0.5	S 2	−2.5
Jupiter	15	4.3	N20	−2.1
Saturn	15	17.7	S 22	+0.7

DECEMBER

Moon	Last 1			New 9
	First 16			Full 23
	Last 31			
Mercury	PM after 19			−0.6
Venus	AM		27°	−3.4
		RA	DEC	MAG
Mars	5	0.5	N 3	−0.6
	15	0.7	N 5	−0.3
	25	1.0	N 7	0.0
Jupiter	15	3.7	N19	−2.3
Saturn	15	18.3	S 23	+0.7
	-o- after 16			

Regulus 10.1^h, N12°; Spica 13.4^h, S11°; Antares 16.5^h, S26°

1989

JANUARY

Moon	New 7			First 14
	Full 21			Last 29
Mercury	PM to 20			+1.5
	AM after 29			+1.9
Venus	AM		20°	−3.3
		RA	DEC	MAG
Mars	5	1.3	N 9	+0.2
	15	1.7	N11	+0.4
	25	2.0	N13	+0.6
Jupiter	15	3.6	N18	−2.2
Saturn	-o- to 7			
	15	18.5	S 23	+0.7

FEBRUARY

Moon	New 6			First 12
	Full 20			Last 28
Mercury	AM			+1.5 to +0.1
Venus	AM		12°	−3.4
	-o- after 23			
		RA	DEC	MAG
Mars	5	2.4	N16	+0.8
	15	2.8	N18	+0.9
	25	3.2	N19	+1.1
Jupiter	15	3.7	N19	−2.0
Saturn	15	18.7	S 22	+0.8

MARCH

Moon	New 7			First 14
	Full 22			Last 30
Mercury	AM to 25			−0.8
Venus			-o-	
		RA	DEC	MAG
Mars	5	3.6	N21	+1.2
	15	4.0	N22	+1.3
	25	4.4	N23	+1.5
Jupiter	15	3.9	N20	−1.8
Saturn	15	18.9	S 22	+0.8

APRIL

Moon	New 5			First 12
	Full 20			Last 28
Mercury	PM after 14			−1.3
Venus			-o-	
		RA	DEC	MAG
Mars	5	4.9	N24	+1.6
	15	5.3	N25	+1.6
	25	5.8	N25	+1.7
Jupiter	15	4.3	N21	−1.6
Saturn	15	19.0	S 22	+0.6

MAY

Moon	New 5			First 12
	Full 20			Last 27
Mercury	PM to 16			+2.4
Venus	PM after 14		11°	−3.4
		RA	DEC	MAG
Mars	5	6.3	N25	+1.8
	15	6.8	N24	+1.9
	25	7.2	N24	+1.9
Jupiter	15	4.7	N22	−1.5
	-o- after 26			
Saturn	15	19.0	S 22	+0.5

JUNE

Moon	New 3			First 11
	Full 19			Last 26
Mercury	AM			+2.4 to −0.3
Venus	PM		18°	−3.3
		RA	DEC	MAG
Mars	5	7.6	N23	+2.0
	15	8.1	N22	+2.0
	25	8.5	N20	+2.0
Jupiter	-o- to 23			
Saturn	15	18.8	S 22	+0.3

Nearby comparison stars (all of magnitude +1.2): Aldebaran 4.6^h, N16°; Pollux 7.7^h, N28°

1989

JULY

Moon	New 3			First 10
	Full 18			Last 25
Mercury	AM to 10			−1.3
	PM after 27			−1.0
Venus	PM		26°	−3.3
		RA	DEC	MAG
Mars	5	9.0	N19	+2.0
	15	9.4	N17	+2.0
	25	9.8	N15	+2.0
Jupiter	15	5.9	N23	−1.5
Saturn	15	18.7	S 22	+0.3

OCTOBER

Moon	First 7			Full 14
	Last 21			New 29
Mercury	AM to 26			−0.9
Venus	PM		46°	−3.8
		RA	DEC	MAG
Mars			-o-	
Jupiter	15	6.8	N23	−1.9
Saturn	15	18.6	S 23	+0.7

AUGUST

Moon	New 1			First 9
	Full 16			Last 23
	New 31			
Mercury	PM			−0.6 to +0.5
Venus	PM		34°	−3.4
		RA	DEC	MAG
Mars	5	10.2	N12	+2.0
	15	10.6	N10	+2.0
	25	11.0	N 7	+2.0
Jupiter	15	6.2	N23	−1.6
Saturn	15	18.6	S 23	+0.4

NOVEMBER

Moon	First 6			Full 13
	Last 19			New 27
Mercury	PM after 29			−0.5
Venus	PM		47°	−4.1
		RA	DEC	MAG
Mars	5	13.9	S 11	+1.9
	15	14.3	S 14	+1.9
	25	14.8	S 16	+1.9
Jupiter	15	6.8	N23	−2.1
Saturn	15	18.8	S 23	+0.8

SEPTEMBER

Moon	First 8			Full 15
	Last 21			New 29
Mercury	PM to 19			+1.7
Venus	PM		41°	−3.6
		RA	DEC	MAG
Mars			-o-	
Jupiter	15	6.6	N23	−1.7
Saturn	15	18.5	S 23	+0.6

DECEMBER

Moon	First 5			Full 12
	Last 19			New 27
Mercury	PM			−0.5 to +0.3
Venus	PM		40°	−4.4
		RA	DEC	MAG
Mars	5	15.2	S 18	+1.9
	15	15.7	S 20	+1.8
	25	16.2	S 21	+1.8
Jupiter	15	6.5	N23	−2.3
Saturn	15	19.0	S 22	+0.7
	-o- after 26			

Regulus 10.1^h, N12°; Spica 13.4^h, S11°; Antares 16.5^h, S26°

1990

JANUARY

Moon	First 4		Full 10
	Last 18		New 26
Mercury	PM to 5		+1.7
	AM after 14		+1.6
Venus	PM to 15		
	AM after 23		

		RA	DEC	MAG
Mars	5	16.7	S 22	+1.7
	15	17.2	S 23	+1.7
	25	17.8	S 24	+1.6
Jupiter	15	6.2	N23	−2.2
Saturn	-o- to 18			

FEBRUARY

Moon	First 2		Full 9
	Last 17		New 25
Mercury	AM		+0.8 to −0.8
Venus	AM	33°	−4.3

		RA	DEC	MAG
Mars	5	18.3	S 24	+1.6
	15	18.9	S 23	+1.5
	25	19.4	S 23	+1.4
Jupiter	15	6.1	N23	−2.1
Saturn	15	19.5	S 22	+0.8

MARCH

Moon	First 3		Full 11
	Last 19		New 26
Mercury	ꓥAM to 6		−0.7
	PM after 28		−1.3
Venus	AM	45°	−4.2

		RA	DEC	MAG
Mars	5	19.8	S 22	+1.4
	15	20.3	S 21	+1.3
	25	20.8	S 19	+1.2
Jupiter	15	6.1	N23	−1.9
Saturn	15	19.7	S 21	+0.8

APRIL

Moon	First 2		Full 9
	Last 18		New 24
Mercury	PM to 26		+2.5
Venus	AM	46°	−3.9

		RA	DEC	MAG
Mars	5	21.4	S 17	+1.2
	15	21.9	S 14	+1.1
	25	22.4	S 12	+1.0
Jupiter	15	6.3	N23	−1.7
Saturn	15	19.6	S 21	+0.7

MAY

Moon	First 1		Full 9
	Last 17		New 24
	First 31		
Mercury	AM after 9		+2.5
Venus	AM	42°	−3.6

		RA	DEC	MAG
Mars	5	22.8	S 9	+0.9
	15	23.3	S 6	+0.9
	25	23.8	S 4	+0.8
Jupiter	15	6.7	N23	−1.5
Saturn	15	19.8	S 21	+0.6

JUNE

Moon	Full 8		Last 15
	New 22		First 29
Mercury	AM to 24		−1.4
Venus	AM	36°	−3.4

		RA	DEC	MAG
Mars	5	0.3	0	+0.6
	15	0.7	N 2	+0.6
	25	1.1	N 5	+0.5
Jupiter	15	7.1	N23	−1.4
Saturn	15	19.7	S 21	+0.4

Nearby comparison stars (all of magnitude +1.2): Aldebaran 4.6^h, N16°; Pollux 7.7^h, N28°

1990

JULY

Moon	Full 7			Last 15
	New 21			First 29
Mercury	PM after 11			−1.0
Venus	AM		29°	−3.3
		RA	DEC	MAG
Mars	5	1.6	N 8	+0.4
	15	2.0	N10	+0.3
	25	2.4	N12	+0.2
Jupiter		-o-		
Saturn	15	19.6	S 22	+0.2

OCTOBER

Moon	Full 4			Last 10
	New 18			First 26
Mercury	AM to 7			−1.1
Venus			-o-	
		RA	DEC	MAG
Mars	5	4.8	N21	−0.8
	15	4.9	N22	−1.1
	25	4.9	N22	−1.3
Jupiter	15	8.9	N18	−1.6
Saturn	15	19.4	S 22	+0.7

AUGUST

Moon	Full 6			Last 13
	New 20			First 28
Mercury	PM			0.0 to +2.4
Venus	AM		21°	−3.3
		RA	DEC	MAG
Mars	5	2.9	N14	+0.1
	15	3.3	N16	0.0
	25	3.7	N18	−0.1
Jupiter	15	8.1	N21	−1.4
Saturn	15	19.4	S 22	+0.4

NOVEMBER

Moon	Full 2			Last 9
	New 17			First 25
Mercury	PM after 6			−0.5
Venus			-o-	
		RA	DEC	MAG
Mars	5	4.8	N23	−1.5
	15	4.5	N23	−1.7
	25	4.3	N23	−1.8
Jupiter	15	9.0	N17	−1.8
Saturn	15	19.5	S 22	+0.8

SEPTEMBER

Moon	Full 4			Last 11
	New 18			First 27
Mercury	AM after 13			+1.6
Venus	AM to 28		13°	−3.4
		RA	DEC	MAG
Mars	5	4.0	N19	−0.3
	15	4.3	N20	−0.5
	25	4.6	N21	−0.6
Jupiter	15	8.5	N19	−1.5
Saturn	15	19.4	S 22	+0.6

DECEMBER

Moon	Full 2			Last 8
	New 16			First 25
	Full 31			
Mercury	PM to 19			+1.7
Venus	PM after 13		11°	−3.4
		RA	DEC	MAG
Mars	5	4.0	N22	−1.6
	15	3.8	N22	−1.3
	25	3.7	N22	−1.0
Jupiter	15	9.1	N17	−2.0
Saturn	15	19.7	S 21	+0.8

Regulus 10.1^h, N12°; Spica 13.4^h, S11°; Antares 16.5^h, S26°

Index